NO MAGIC

Readings in Social Work Field Education

edited by
Gail L. Kenyon
and
Roxanne Power

Canadian Scholars' Press Inc.   Toronto   2000

No Magic: Readings in Social Work Field Education
edited by Gail L. Kenyon and Roxanne Power

First published in 2000 by
Canadian Scholars' Press Inc.
180 Bloor Street West, Suite 1202
Toronto, Ontario
M5S 2V6

CSPI acknowledges the financial support of the Government of Canada through the Book Publishing Industry Development Programme for our publishing activities.

Canadian Cataloguing in Publication Data

No Magic: Readings in Social Work Field Education

ISBN 1-55130-165-2

Edited collection of papers from the second Canadian-International Conference on Field Education in Social Work, sponsored by the School of Social Work, McMaster University, Hamilton, Ont. in spring, 1996

1. Social work education – Congresses. 2. Social service – Field work – Congresses. 3. Field work (Educational method) – Congresses. I. Kenyon, Gail L. (Gail Louise), 1951– . II. Power, Roxanne, 1951– . III. Canadian-International Conference on Field Education in Social Work (2nd: 1996: McMaster University). IV. McMaster University, School of Social Work.

HV 11.N62 2000   361.3'071'55   C00-931556-X

Managing Editor: Ruth Bradley-St-Cyr
Marketing Manager: Susan Cuk
Copyediting: Linda Bissinger
Production Editor: Linda Bissinger
Page layout: Brad Horning

Printed and bound in Canada by AGVM Marquis

*This book is dedicated to the memory
of our valued colleague*

*Susan J. O'Neil
Co-ordinator of Field Education
at
King's College
University of Western Ontario
1991 - 1996*

Contents

SECTION III
LINKAGES & EXCHANGES BETWEEN FIELD SETTINGS AND THE UNIVERSITY

Acknowledgements

The co-editors would like to thank Sheila Sammon and Joan Leeson, fellow field co-ordinators who helped in the inception of this project. Many thanks are due to all the readers who reviewed papers and offered helpful suggestions and encouragement. Special thanks is extended to Fran Morphy at Ryerson whose diligent reading found text and numerical errors and who patiently prepared every revision. Many thanks are also due to Ellen Sue Mesbur, who worked with us on polishing the final manuscript over many months. We are grateful for her support and her introduction for this book. Finally, but most importantly, thank you to the authors who endured a lengthy process to get us here. We are proud to be associated with you.

Introduction

Magic is defined as: "the art which claims to control and manipulate the secret forces of nature by occult and ritualistic methods; the practice of this art; any mysterious power or phenomenon which defies analysis or explanation" (Webster, 1988). Rather than magical powers, learning the profession of social work requires a strong foundation of knowledge and theory and a repertoire of skills and methods, grounded in values and ethics that guide social work practice. As field educators, our knowledge and experience take the learning of social work practice from the realm of the supernatural to the known.

This edited collection of articles on field education, from the perspective of field educators in academia and the field, is representative of the juried papers and presentations that comprised the second Canadian-International Conference on Field Education in Social Work, sponsored by the School of Social Work, McMaster University, Hamilton, Ontario in the spring of 1996. The first Canadian-International conference, held in Calgary, Alberta in 1994, resulted in publication of **Social Work Field Education: Views and Visions**, edited by Gayla Rogers.

No Magic: Readings in Social Work Field Education represents some of the current research and teaching developments undertaken by field educators from across North America. Schneck (1995) eloquently describes the essence of field education today when he notes: "In field education, we are uniquely positioned to observe, speculate, and collaborate with our practice colleagues and to shape workable responses to real problems of real people in real times. In a way, our success in field education will presage what's ahead for the rest of society as we strive to promote a cooperative or 'communitarian' ethic for our large urban areas and smaller communities and rural areas as well" (p. 4).

This book reflects Schneck's hope for collaborative efforts in field education. It is organized into three themes. Section I: Contemporary Challenges in Field Education, begins with Gail Kenyon's study of the ways in which field instructors integrate theory into their teaching of students in the field practicum. Kenyon's work, which also sets the theme for the book's title, maintains that social work theory is an important part of the field education experience and that students and field instructors do, in fact, draw upon theory to inform their practice. Patrick Clifford contributes an interesting field teaching methodology using post constructionist and narrative approaches in working with clients. He maintains that field educators must prepare the future generation of social workers to engage clients in rediscovering or finding their own power through the client's context of meaning. The final article in this section, authored by Paul Cappuccio, focuses on the present and future roles for social work in medical settings. Cappuccio examines the demands and realities of Program Management and considers the implications these have for social workers. He maintains that, more than ever, the roots of social work's core functions must be maintained in medical settings to protect and enhance the unique nature of hospital social work practice.

Section II: Approaches to Field Education Delivery, highlights four creative contributions to field education. Gayla Rogers and Barbara Thomlison present a study of the preferred learning styles of social work students and their use of documentation tools to facilitate learning in the field practicum. The linking of learning tools to learning styles sets the foundation for future curriculum development, particularly in relation to the differential use of documentation tools. In their description of an interdisciplinary student seminar program, Nona Moscovitz and Helen Szewello Allen illustrate the richness of a partnership between a community agency and an academic institution in the development and implementation of a structured educational program in a field setting. Emerging from the results of massive restructuring of social services in Quebec, this program met the learning and teaching needs of students and field instructors and has contributed to knowledge-building in models for field education. A group supervision program, as described by Jeanne Michaud, builds on and complements individual supervision of students. Ongoing group meetings provide rich opportunities for the sharing of different practice experiences and theories and for the further development of self-awareness in an atmosphere of mutual support. The final article in this section by Glen Schmidt reports on the challenges of creating a field education program in remote and isolated settings in northwestern Canada. Rural based practice differs from urban based practice, not only in the availability of services and resources, but also in the nature of social work practice itself. Building upon current field education knowledge, the field education program was established in the "hinterland" through strong community partnerships, with flexibility and creative problem-solving as the cornerstones. Interestingly, evaluation results highlight the commonalities of field education regardless of location: the need for regular and consistent communication with agency field instructors, the reality of high practicum turnover during the placement recruitment process, the necessity for additional faculty involvement in the field education process, and the need for clear goals, consistent organization and collaborative approaches.

Section III, Linkages and Exchanges Between Field Settings and the University, highlights the potential for enhancing collaborative opportunities between the academic and practice settings. Judith Globerman and Marion Bogo describe a partnership model that enhances social work education through the integration of research, teaching and practice in graduate programs. The model emphasizes the consulting role of the faculty field liaison, particularly with respect to knowledge building and the integration of practice with research and teaching and the development of inter-organizational relationships. The use of a competency-based curriculum in child welfare field placement settings is the focus of Sherrill Clark and Kathleen McCormick's article in this section. A competency-based curriculum for graduate students was established through a state-wide, multi-school process with the goals of articulating core competencies and designing opportunities for students that will contribute to their learning. In the final article, Ron Levin, Margot Herbert, and Butch Nutter report on a survey of Canadian Field Education Co-ordinators in schools of social work to determine their perceptions of recent changes in hospitals or other health settings on the field practicum. The results illustrate the need for schools of social work to implement changes in academic curriculum to reflect the current realities of social work practice. While the study focused specifically on health care settings, the themes of change permeate virtually all practice settings and have considerable implications for the future of social work education.

This collection of scholarly work represents some of the latest and most innovative approaches to field education and contributes significantly to the future of social work field education.

Ellen Sue Mesbur, MSW, Ed. D.
School of Social Work
Ryerson Polytechnic University

References

Schneck, D. (1995). The promise of field education in social work. In G. Rogers (Ed.), *Social work field education: Views and visions* (pp. 3-14). Dubuque, Iowa: Kendall/Hunt.

The New Lexicon Webster's Encyclopedic Dictionary of the English Language, Canadian Edition (1988). New York: Lexicon Publications, Inc.

SECTION I

CONTEMPORARY CHALLENGES IN FIELD INSTRUCTION

Chapter 1

No Magic:
The Role of Theory in Field Education

Gail L. Kenyon

The integration of theory into practice is an expectation placed on practicum instructors by schools and faculties of social work across the country. It is rarely challenged as an important part of the practicum training for social work students. Most field education manuals list it as an important role for the field instructor to fulfil.

In their widely used book *The Practice of Field Instruction in Social Work Theory and Process* (1986), Bogo and Vayda talk about the "linkage" component of their "integration of theory and practice" loop (p. 4). They state: "Schools across Canada present to students a variety of theories and practice models which may include systems theory, developmental theory, role theory, social change theory, or a structural analysis of social systems" (p.4). They emphasize that "the field instructor's task is not only to draw the student's attention to theoretical knowledge but also to help the student apply that knowledge in relation to a specific practice situation" (p. 4). However, in my experience as a practicum co-ordinator and in discussions with practicum co-ordinators from other schools, I have begun to suspect that this task is difficult for practicum instructors to carry out properly and that students seldom experience an ideal situation.

To gather further information on this important topic, I set out to interview both field instructors and students in a masters-level social work program. I used the method proposed by Glaser and Strauss (1967), which outlines the process for discovering grounded theory. This method proposes that theory be arrived at through the data rather than beginning with *a priori* assumptions and setting out to prove or disprove them. The grounded theory approach and other naturalistic methods of inquiry produce what Glaser and Strauss call "theory suited to its supposed uses" (1967, p. 3). The goal is to develop conceptual categories that arise from the data collected.

I began by interviewing three practitioners who had been identified by the practicum director of the graduate-level program at a faculty of social work. These practioners were identified as experienced field instructors who exhibited a good understanding of the educational role of the practicum, which proved to be true. All three had had many students and were clearly dedicated to the educational role of the practicum. I went into each interview with three broad questions: "What are your thoughts about integrating theory into practice in your practicum instruction?"; "How do you go about doing that?"; and "Are there suggestions you would give to practicum instructors who are struggling with this task?". These questions were asked in a variety of ways within the flow of the interview, but all were covered with each respondent. Each interview was audiotaped and transcribed for analysis. The transcripts were read and reread to find several emerging themes. The following themes recurred in all respondents.

The Party Line

Each respondent was eager to inform me that they agreed with the university about the importance of integrating theory into practice. They opened the interview with statements such as: "I think it is extremely important to do,"and "It takes a particular focus on theory on the part of the supervisor to maintain that as an integral piece of the supervision." One field instructor related the importance to my interview: "I am glad to see this research being done. I think it is an important area of work that maybe there is not enough effort put into."

While the enthusiasm may have been a reflection of their true thoughts, it may also have been what they wanted the university to hear, as I was probably viewed as an agent of the university. It is also important to note that some respondents followed these statements of the party line with the reason that they could not meet this expectation, even though it was important. The reasons included: "Sometimes it's difficult to do, you know, because you get students here who have cases, just managing the day to day, often times just takes over … ," and "I can't give specific examples, I mean, I haven't done all the reading."

No Magic

Another theme was that social work is not magic. It can be learned. It is not an intuitive process but is based on theory and learned skills. One statement reflects the attitude of the field instructors: "I really encourage the students to try to do their work based on knowledge and theory rather than just being intuitive about it … there is really no magic to it." Another field instructor says: "It's not magic, I tell them, you can learn this as well as anybody else," and "I have information and it's not magic, I've learned it, somebody else can learn it too."

Role of the University

The practicum instructors interviewed used material provided by the university and appreciated the help that was offered. Sometimes they indicated that they would like the faculty to provide more help for them in this difficult task, possibly by sharing articles, or making the professors' orientations known to the field instructors: "Sometimes what would be helpful for me, I guess, would be to know some of the new professors and get a sense of what they are teaching and what they want emphasized." "Something that would be really helpful would be if there is really a key article that comes around on supervising students, different things that have been tried that have been really helpful, it would be good to have that information."

Student Level

The level of the student was often cited as an important factor in the integration of theory into practice. More mature, skilled students were more able to do this task. Beginning students were still focussed on basic skills and, therefore, could not be expected to be integrating theory to the same extent. One student was seen as "operating at a fairly high level in terms of her interventions because all the easy stuff she had 'hands down.'" Another student could "start out at a fairly significant level." This student was seen as more able to integrate theory and, in fact, could do that on her own.

Students do it Themselves

An important theme was that students actually provide the integration of theory into practice for themselves. Students who could bring theory into the field instruction meeting and apply it themselves were seen as good and exceptional students. "X was an interesting student, she herself would sort of be able to say, 'I think that based on blah, blah, blah, that the timing was right,' or she just came with what she had read, something that made sense to her. She was really solid at saying 'that doesn't make sense to me and I'm reading ... that was just wonderful and I learned so much.'" In fact, students are seen as a source of learning for the field instructor: "Students will often share some of their learning. I like to read their essays."

Methods

In the interviews, I tried to get a clear picture of what methods field instructors used to teach the integration of theory into practice. One common method of integration used course outlines to match student practicum activities with the areas covered in the course. Another field instructor shared handouts she had received from the school or had the student bring in articles that could then be discussed in relation to the student's cases.

There was one very good example of the field instructor and the student working together to find the theoretical knowledge they needed to proceed with a case that dealt with issues new to both of them:

> Well it turns out that neither of us had the theoretical background we needed to be helpful. We could either refer out, or we could try to figure out what we could do. So there was a real scramble to consult with people who had worked in that area with much more intensity than we had, to do a pile of literature search and then read, which we did as a twosome.

Integration of Theory into Practice

However, the field instructors were rarely able to give me clear examples of instances where they had suggested theoretical concepts to the student and discussed with them how that might help the student in understanding a case or planning an intervention. There was the occasional example of integration: "... then I talk a bit about crisis theory and sometimes you have to be more directive in helping people deal with a crisis." Another field instructor was able to describe what might happen: "There might be some information that I might have on object relations and how that might be applied to work with a client in, say, parenting issues ... theory has specific techniques which enhance student's skills. Therefore the student would understand how to apply that skill to a specific client and then could generalize that knowledge to other clients." But this was hypothetical. Overall the interviews lacked examples of instructors assisting students in integrating theory into their practice.

In addition, there were several instances where opportunities to do this type of teaching of integration were missed. The student would be discussing a client or situation and the field instructor would miss the opportunity to draw out of that situation how various theories might have informed the student's work. In describing to the interviewer a discussion with a student (X) of how the student might change the direction she was taking with a female client, the field instructor indicated: "I try not to be too intervening. Finally, I said, 'You know, X, I think that all that insight and sort of letting go of that relationship she (the client) used to have ... right now she needs to kick that guy she's living with out and sort of get on with things.'" This was a situation where the field instructor could have introduced theory to help the student modify her treatment plan if necessary. There were other opportunities missed as well. In talking with her student about a particular case the field instructor noted: "... you have got to be able to move beyond making excuses to me about why you're not pushing these people a little bit ...." The field instructor could have named the theoretical construct for the student and discussed how that might apply to the situation, but this did not happen. Generally the field instructors did not give examples of teaching the integration of theory into practice and they seemed not to take advantage of opportunities to do this type of teaching.

If you are looking for your car keys in the kitchen and do not find them how do you know if you are successful and they are not there or if you have failed and just could not find them. These were dedicated skilled practicum instructors, but they were clearly having difficulty meeting the expectations of the university. Although they wanted to integrate theory into their students' practice and espoused the value of doing so, they were not able to give examples of this happening. Was the problem that this type of teaching was not happening, or was I just not able to uncover it with my method of inquiry?

Dr. Nick Coady (1995) argues that a "positivistic, technical-rational philosophy in social work has obscured the fact that practice is primarily a reflective/inductive process" (p. 139). He also cites Schon (1983) in a study of five professions (engineering, architecture, management, town planning and psychotherapy). Schon states that much of professional practice does not involve the application of established theory and technique. Rather, he suggested that most professional practice involves what he calls "knowing-in-action" and "reflection-in-action" (p. 141). "Knowing-in-action" is defined by Schon (1983) as "spontaneous behaviour of skilful practice ... which does not stem from a prior intellectual operation" (p. 51). "Reflection-in-action," as the name connotes, involves "thinking on your feet" (Coady, 1995, p. 141). Schon states that when someone is reflecting-in-action, "He is not dependent on categories of established theory and technique but constructs a new theory of the unique case.... He does not separate thinking from doing, ratiocinating his way to a decision which he must later convert to action.... Thus reflection-in-action can proceed, even in situations of uncertainty or uniqueness" (Schon, 1983, p. 68). One other concept from Schon (1987) seems relevant. He talks about "theories-in-use," defining the concept as a kind of knowing-in-action that is constructed by "reflecting on the directly observable data of our actual interpersonal practice" (p. 256). These theories include "values, strategies, and underlying assumptions" (p.255). Could it be that formal theory, like other life experience and learning, is integrated into the practitioners' knowing and is expressed as part of the theory-in-use?

In reviewing the data in the light of this new view of integration I found hints. Field instructors talked about "gut feelings;" "they (the students) don't realize that they know something really well;" "what they did even though they didn't know it was theory;" "I am not sure whether it was the intervention or the way the student was, it is hard to separate that out, probably a combination of both, but she just had an excellent rapport with this client;" "Some of it you do intuitively, and sort of learn all the time;" and even allowing the student to say, "That doesn't make sense to me; I'm not about to do that."

I re-examined the missed opportunities I had identified before.

> Field Instructor: I try not to do too much intervening. Finally I said, "You know X (the social work student) I think that all that insight and sort of letting go of that relationship (the client) used to have ... right now she needs to kick that guy she's living with out and (laugh) get on with things. Her relationship with her mother might take a natural course and sort itself out, but we're just wallowing in this kind of poor me, she didn't love me. Why try to deal with mom? She only has to see mom by choice, she doesn't live with her but she lives with this guy day after day, why don't we focus on the reality of getting her strong enough to make a decision to either give him some rules of the road or (throw him) out". I think X herself was feeling that she was going around in circles with it and getting frustrated .... I would talk about different styles and how I think insight therapy probably works for people who basically aren't in crisis, and can get on with their day-to-day life. But if you're in crisis, let's deal with that. Then I talk a little bit about crisis theory and sometimes you have to be more interventionist, more directive.

I was forced to ask whether this field instructor was helping the student modify her theory-in-use. Perhaps this was integration in action, and not just a rather weak example of integration of theory into practice. Grounded theory warns that the answers respondents give can be limited by the conceptualization of the question. I had to rethink the question that I had been asking. What is the purpose of theory in practice? It is to allow the practitioner to formulate a hypothesis about the situation and then help in decision making regarding the direction the process should take. The more appropriate question to ask field instructors and their students is how do they teach and learn that skill. To explore this idea I interviewed two students who were at the end of their degree and, therefore, had completed two placement experiences each at the graduate level. This time I asked the original questions: "What are your thoughts about integrating theory into practice in your practicum instruction?" and "What has been your experience of that?" And I added a broader question: "How do you learn to make sense of a given situation or problem and figure out what to do next?"

In response to the first question the students confirmed the data collected from the field instructors. They had received almost none of what I will now call the formal integration of academic theory into practice. One student stated: "What I found was it was sort of my responsibility to put the two together.... that was something that I was responsible to figure out how to go about doing."

They spoke of feeling that it was up to them to integrate theory and that their field instructor was not going to help them: "As far as sitting down and talking a lot about, well, what does so and so say about this and then how would you go about doing that in a session ... that was something that was up to me to do;" and "... I was hoping that I would learn from him how to do this and that was where ... it was a bit of rude awakening for me to realize, oh, if I want to do this stuff then I'm gonna have to do it on my own."

Even when the field instructor had a very definite theoretical orientation it was not always offered directly to the student as an example of how theory might inform their practice. Sometimes it was used extensively in field instruction as with the student whose field instructor spent a lot of supervision time talking about the transference issues between student and practicum instructor and only after many weeks, suggested this might also be applicable to a situation between the student and one of her clients: "he'll say something like, 'well we've been struggling over our relationship issue, you know, supervisor-supervisee relationship for the past two and a half months. Did you ever consider that what's happening between you and this particular client ... was parallel?'"

Another field instructor was able to link the theoretical and methodological perspective adopted by the agency to the student's work with her clients. However, she was not able to make links with other theoretical perspectives and doggedly persisted in the application of the agency-adopted theory even though the client had rejected it and the field instructor herself had conceded that "it doesn't work with everybody."

The place where academic theory was integrated into practice was through the family practice class at the university. When assigned the task of applying an academic theory to a family they had worked with, students found the theory worked very well to explain both the client's situation and the treatment or intervention choices they had made. This was done in hindsight as the student linked theory with intervention and outcome.

However, the most important data came from the student response to the second question: "How do you learn to make sense of a given situation or problem and figure out what to do next?" Several themes emerged.

Winging It

The students consistently doubted their own abilities and talked about "winging it," or "flying by the seat of my pants" and used other euphemisms for responding intuitively, or without formal theory consciously applied. These examples abound: "I think I felt a little bit like I was flying by the seat of my pants, in terms of putting theory into practice. I just tried to be myself and see what came out of that;" "I flew by the seat of my pants at times;" "I was just kind of going along, I always call it 'winging it;'" and "When you are a beginning counsellor, just try and wing it without much theory." When something worked really well they attributed it to chance: "Luck was in my favour."

However, far from having no notion of what to do, both students demonstrated two things. They consistently had a very well-developed theory about each client or situation they worked with. These were demonstrated in detailed examples of their work with clients or communities. Secondly, they both were developing a theory of practice, an overarching model of how practice actually worked.

Theory-In-Use

The examples of their work with cases demonstrated that the students had developed a detailed working understanding of the client and their life situation. This was apparent as one student described both the client's situation, and his/her own thinking and planning regarding the case.

> Student: There was one particular family that I worked with, the presenting problem was a five year old boy. It was a single mom that came, she was quite young, and she came with her son and her mother. She had been married briefly, her husband had been abusive towards her and they decided to divorce. The father was still involved with the child on a regular basis,

and her mother was also quite actively involved. Her mother was a widow and often took care of the child for her when she would work. She was like a second mother in a way, the grandmother ... The school was getting really fed-up with him [the child] because he was so aggressive. They were calling home every day and saying come get him because they can't control him. She (his mother) was getting blamed ... she can't control her kid, she's a terrible mother and also having gotten some of these messages from her ex-husband, she just, her body language, everything about her was so down, you could just read it on her face, she looked so sad and down and felt nothing good about herself in her skills as a mother or even as a person ... Her mother, who at first seemed to really be a strong support for her and would appear to be really helpful, was really reinforcing some of those negatives. She was constantly putting her (daughter) down, correcting if she tried to mother in a certain way. She would criticize her and tell her she was doing it wrong and then the grandmother tried to get me on her side, (saying) don't you think that a boy should really go to bed by eight o'clock and I think the problem is that she's not spending enough time with him. I just thought oh, my goodness. I could see that (it was) no wonder that this woman's not effective as a parent, I mean there was all these generational things beating her down more and more and more, and then the son, who was only five was just becoming, in my eyes, so powerful because this grandmother just adored him, he could do no wrong. And I could see that the grandmother probably thought she was being helpful. Having recently lost her husband, I think that she felt this was an important role for her to do. She could be important in this little boy's life. But it was very hard on her daughter. I tried to do a little bit of structural work, physically. They would come into the office and the grandmother would take the boy on her lap and, in the middle of the session she'd be reading him a story as if to say aren't I just a wonderful grandmother. I had just huge counter-transference, I was starting to really hate this woman. I tried to put some space ... I would have the mother sit with the child and try to put some space with me between the grandmother. She was certainly important in his life but there was a clear boundary there. And I used a lot of the strength perspective, I don't know if you would consider that a model per se. The child was very active and he was all over and aggressive and so right in the session she would have to attend to him, and I would comment on anything she did that was effective, because she was often effective in the session. It was clear that she could do it, she could have him sit down and she would hug him and do things that would help him calm down and I would just comment on it. My supervisor observed through the mirror and every time I said something positive about her (the child's mother), it was like she just came to life, she started standing, sitting up straighter, she looked up, her face just lit up. And I started talking about how hard it must be for her, she must really love her son a lot because she is working so hard and how great it was that they had been able to work out this arrangement between the two of them to give the grandmother some support. Clearly I was giving the message that (the grandmother) was not his mother, and that there was a boundary there that she was assisting her, that her role was clearly not to be in charge, which I think was really hard for her (the grandmother) to hear. Initially the mother would always look to her mother before saying anything. She wouldn't even be able to speak directly, she would always look to her as if to say answer for me or is it okay that I say this, or I don't know what exactly she was thinking. Eventually, she was able to at least speak directly to me and not be, you know, filtering through this woman.

The student demonstrated excellent ability to make meaning out the information given to her by her clients and from her observation. Theory building can be seen each time she makes an interpretation of this information: for example, describing the grandmother as "like a second mother," or the mother "(she) felt nothing good about herself in her skills as a mother or even as a person." She then uses this inductively arrived at theory to make decisions regarding action, such as: "I would comment on anything she (the mother) did that was effective." The student uses formal academic theory to explain her decisions after the fact: "I tried to do a bit of kind of structural work."

Another example demonstrates when the student makes a theory-in-use that does not work very well. The intervention of the field instructor helps the student modify her theory and make better intervention decisions.

> Student: See, my gut was telling me listen I'm not gonna get anywhere and I'm getting frustrated, and I didn't know at that point to talk about my frustration with her (the client). So my supervisor suggested to me, why don't you talk about the frustration that you're experiencing with her when she says 'don't know, don't care', because that probably parallels the frustration that her parents feel with her, or that anyone else who talks to her when she clams up like that feels. So I got her back and I started talking about that and eventually our relationship was just amazing. That was a reaction that I took (to terminate the client), that was a gut reaction. I had just had it with her but now I know more to listen to what's happening, that's what I'm talking about my gut feeling, maybe I should have tried talking about my frustration first rather than just letting her go. And then that's when I started thinking about other things too. How can I connect with this girl, because obviously I'm having a connection problem. So I thought up some ideas like, have her sit in the supervisor's chair and me sit in the client chair. The other thought I had was maybe she needs to draw, maybe she needs a pad of paper in front of her or something that she can do while talking to me, or maybe we should just play cards and get connected first. I was pushing things to understand what was happening in her life and meanwhile we hadn't even gotten connected yet.

The student was able to take the field instructor's suggested modification to her theory about this client and implement it in her next session with the client. Understanding the client's resistance as a reaction to their lack of relationship helped the student change the focus of her work and be creative in looking at strategies to move forward.

Theory of Practice

Each student talked at length about their developing understanding of what was important in practice, what worked and what their role was. It seemed that they were spontaneously developing a theory about social work practice. The later part of this example is a description of inductive theory building:

> A lot of it is being yourself, and doing what makes sense and giving of yourself. That's a big part of it. I do believe that my natural way of being is probably helpful but it's not the whole picture. You can't just be there and expect that to be the intervention. But that did help a lot, those qualities doing all the things that don't really belong to any one theory, re-framing and ... those things that probably everyone does but maybe I was a little bit more familiar with because I didn't feel married to any one theory at that point. I felt like I've got all this stuff swimming around in my head, and I'm sure it comes out without even realizing some of the stuff. It's kind of a big mishmash of theory.

In this instance the student is developing a model for how social work intervention actually takes place — with action, reflection, assessment and planning:

> You know, wing it first and then analyse it later, then you can decide where you're gonna go after you've analysed that first trick or whichever direction you decided to go in your gut. And after the session, you can think about, well, did that work or did that not work and if it didn't work then we have to decide what approach we're gonna take next time.

At the same time the students built guiding principles for their practice:

> I believe that people know what's best for them .... To respect that they're gonna go in whatever direction they're gonna go. And if they don't go in any direction, well, then that's fine too, because that's their choice."

To consolidate these findings, I went back to a field instructor to see what response I would get to the broader conceptual question: "How do you teach your student to make sense of the client's situation and know what to do next?" Rather than re-interview a field instructor, I sought out one who was relatively new to the job. The presumption might be that she was closer to the theory she learned in class and, therefore, more likely to integrate formal academic theory into practice. I began the interview by asking the original question regarding the integration of theory into practice. This field instructor responded exactly as the previous field instructor interviewees had responded: "I think it is really important ..." and "I tell the students that I think it's important that they integrate theory into their practice ...." This was followed shortly after by the reason that this was hard to do: "It's just a matter of time .... We have an hour, sometimes an hour-and-a-half, whatever we can afford, if there's things happening, there's crises here all the time so ...." Several other themes identified earlier also could be seen. The "no magic" theme was addressed in an interesting way. While the students thought that if something good happened it was luck or chance, this field instructor, like the others, did not agree. When making decisions about a case she jokes: "I never toss a coin." She too thought student level was relevant and was pleased to have had two very capable students. She also gave examples of the students bringing the theory with them and applying it themselves to cases they carried. Two experiences of learning from the student were also recounted.

However, it became apparent very quickly that what the university saw as integrating theory into practice was not happening in the field instruction sessions. In response to the question, "Do you link specific theory with the student?" the field instructor replied:

> I'm trying to think of how many times we do that when we speak. Not particularly, not in generalities. We have our own assessment model that we utilize ... but no, we don't usually get right down into specific theories. A lot of our theory here is from ... we utilize a lot of things from a lot of different theories, like systems for analysing family dynamics and group theory, but I don't really get too specific.

Later she said: "I don't ask them (the students) to say what clinician said that and where did you get that from," and again later, she refers to naming specific theories as "getting nit-picky about who said what and when, no, I don't do that."

Having confirmed the data from the first three field instructors, I moved on to the broader question: "How do you teach your students to understand what is going on with the clients and make decisions about what to do next?" The responses were congruent with the student responses. Excellent examples were given:

> Field Instructor: I do that through discussion, and I try to put it back on the student. I'm not gonna sit here and say you need to do this or that. You have to also look at this as a child protection agency, so we have to go back to brass tacks. Is the child safe? We work from there. I generally start with the risk to the child and if, yes, there is risk to the child then you would ask what can we do as an agency to help ensure this child's not going to be injured again, and what does this mom or dad need. I'm trying to think of when she (the student) came back from that visit, we talked about the risk to the child and where mom is coming from, mom's family of origin and the supports that mom had and then we made a plan. Do we need to be involved? What are the services that this lady might need? Does she need referrals or that sort of thing? This particular student did work with that woman and did very well in that situation. But I try to really have the student participate in the learning and in the decision making. I don't think you learn a whole lot coming and sitting down and your supervisor tells you exactly what and when and why and how and do it now (laugh), so I like more of a participation approach.

The field instructor is describing the process she uses to teach the student how to assess a situation and make the relevant intervention decisions. She becomes even more specific about how a student might do that on a home visit:

> Field Instructor: Yeah, the student was able to look at who the child was and how old the child was and was there any injury? It was a slap and there wasn't any mark. Then (she) look(ed) at mom and where mom is at and how did mom present, was

mom remorseful? This particular lady was extremely remorseful, she was feeling so bad she reported herself. So, she looked at individual issues with the child and individual issues with the mom and she looked at the global environment around supports and also the pressures in this woman's life. She (the mom) was back in school and on financial assistance and not real happy about that, but happy to be back in school. The student also looked at things that would relieve the mom's stress. So I remember her going through all of that and then us going back to our mandate and saying what can we do for this lady at this particular time. That's sort of how we made a decision on what the plan was going to be for the next few weeks of her involvement with this woman. The student did most of that actually.

This is teaching the student how to build a theory about this unique case. There is no discussion of specific academic theory; however, the field instructor is able to help the student begin to understand this client and her situation and make tentative decisions about intervention. The field instructor describes the process further: "So, basically, you know, she (the student) would do something with a client and bring it back to me and tell me what she had done. And (the students) also talk about the results of that, I mean not everything you do with a client works, you know, and then we talk about different ways of doing things …."

This is not "winging-it" nor is it "magic." It appears to be a methodical process based on social work skills and principles. Neither is it the imposition of a particular academic theory selected by the field instructor or by the agency. The field instructor is able to teach the student how to build a inductive theory and then explore that theory with the student. If it is not working, the field instructor offers possible modifications to theory.

In reflecting on the process for teaching this to students, the field instructor begins to elaborate on her own theory of practice, and of field instruction:

… they're the ones who were at the door and met the people and they're the ones who've had that experience, so you really need to encourage them. How did you feel about that? What did you observe? What did the person say? What did you say to them? So there's a lot of interaction between me and the student and talking about that.

She asks the student to recount the process the student used to understand the client and the client's situation: "... tell me what happened today, and tell me what went on, and what do you think has made this person do this ...."

What is the role of academic theory then? When asked this question the field instructor used an example to reply:

> ... One of my students in particular had a lot of knowledge around offenders and around the personality of an offender and what their behavioural characteristics are, also around abuse and wife assault, and clearly she was clinically right on target with that. In discussing a sexual abuse case, we were able to talk about that and talk about the dynamics of sexual abuse and offending behaviour. That's where something like that would fit ....

Academic theory informs the student's knowledge about a particular client or situation. It also helps in writing reports, and it is taught by the university:

> In one particular case each of them (the students) had to do what we call a closing assessment, and I had them do the assessment on things like attachment and bonding. Clearly that's something that you need to have at school before you can come here, or go on placement ....

There is no question that formal, academic theory is in use in this setting. However, it is not articulated to the student: "I don't name theories per se ...." One of the best descriptions of "theory-building" and the utilization of "theory-in-use" comes from a particular academic theorist used by the field instructor and in the teaching of child welfare investigation techniques:

> FI: I'm trying to think of what else I do. A lot of thinking (laugh).
> gk: Tell me about the thinking. Where does that fit?
> FI: Well, in abuse, it fits in an hypothesis, you have your various hypotheses and you look at different situations that could

have caused this particular allegation. Then you think about what fits and what doesn't fit and you can conclude generally from that what the decision is around the abuse and whether it occurred.

gk: And when do you do that thinking? When in the process does that actually happen?

FI: The hypothesis should be right from the beginning.

gk: Right from the start.

FI: Yeah, right from the initial call.

gk: Okay. Even before you go out, the first, just right from the first information.

FI: Yeah.

gk: And does it change, often?

FI: The hypothesis?

gk: Yeah.

FI: It can. You can have them added or subtracted from, but it's important to have various hypotheses, you know, I mean initially you start with did it happen or didn't it happen and what you know, we have a child making a statement, but we also have a serious custody battle or we have a statement that could be not sexual intent but somebody was bathing somebody and touched them, not as sexual abuse, but as an act of hygiene, so you have all your different hypotheses. Then as you investigate and you're thorough and .. you do the supervisory process and good investigative skills and generally you should be able to get it down to something (laugh).

gk: The word hypothesis, is that your word or does that come from some source?

FI: It comes from the Raskin.

gk: From Raskin.

FI: Raskin, yeah.. I'm trying to think of his name ... I've lost it, it's German, the whole style of the Raskin model of interviewing came from Germany actually, and using the various hypotheses .... And basically what you do is you eliminate them as you go along, you know. The key, of course, is the interview with the child, and that's why it's important that people are well trained and they know what they're doing when they're interviewing a child.

This interchange demonstrates that this field instructor uses a model for her investigations that closely follows what she is teaching the students. It is based on academic or formal theory. However, even with my asking about the source, it is hard for the field instructor to remember the name of the theorist. The academic theory is integrated into her way of working, her "doing" and her way of teaching her students, and is not easily retrieved or separated from practice.

Conclusions

Having interviewed three field instructors, two students and then an additional field instructor, I concluded that there are several separate processes going on at the same time. The field instructors are trying to meet the stated school objective of integrating theory into practice. They find this difficult for a variety of reasons. Firstly, they do not always have the time or resources to keep up with new theories or changes in existing theories. Secondly, and most importantly, the model this proposes is not easily compatible with the way that they or their students work. Academic theory is integrated into their "doing" to an extent that makes it difficult to extract it for the students.

The other more successful process involves teaching students an inductive/reflective model of working that comes very naturally to both students and practitioners. The student is assessed to see what level of basic social work skill development they have achieved. The field instructor works to bring that skill to a beginning level through practice, supervision and modelling, so that the student can join with their clients, demonstrate empathy and good listening skills. Then the field instructor helps the student develop their own inductive/reflective skills of work. This involves gathering information from the client and formulating a theory-in-use based on that information and what the student already knows (academic theory integrated into the student's "doing," previous work and life experience, etc.) . During field instruction and between meetings with the client, the student reflects on this theory-in-use, compares it to known academic theory, and thinks about it in relation to life experiences, previous cases, etc. The theory-in-use is developing even when the student is not with the client. This new revised theory-in-use is then taken into the next meeting with the client, tested against new information, and revised if necessary. It is from this theory that the student determines the intervention or "what to do next."

Rather than "winging it" or "flying by the seat of their pants," students are constantly drawing on their own bodies of knowledge and skill that have already been integrated into their practice and responding spontaneously in the practice session or meeting. This is not to say that just because the student or practitioner does it, it is right or best for the client. On the contrary this model places the responsibility on the student and practitioner to continue to learn and reflect so as to keep his or her reflective/ inductive skills honed.

The role of the field instructor then becomes that of a skilled practitioner sharing the benefit of his/her more extensive body of integrated knowledge. She also must help the student understand the process of developing inductive theory regarding each case or community situation. As we see with the last field instructor interviewee, the field instructor can teach the student very specific skills for building a theory and then can monitor the student's progress with that theory in field instruction sessions. When the theory fails to work as well as expected, the field instructor can help the student explore alternate theories that could be built from the information the student has or help the student modify her present theory-in-use.

To help students in their own development of a theory of practice, it would be beneficial for the field instructor to make the process of inductive theory building explicit. In this way students are less mystified about the process and have less doubt about what they are doing. The students can see their own skill level and build on that as they go.

Academic theory is one more source of knowledge that can be used by practitioners in their work. This theory can come from the student to the field instruction setting, from the field instructor to the student, or it can be something that they seek out together to inform a particular theory-in-use.

Although further study is required, it appears that schools and faculties of social work may be more helpful to their students and their field instructors by providing concrete information about academic theories in the form of articles and handouts. At the same time both students and field instructors would feel more successful if a reflective/inductive model of theory building was introduced both in the classroom and in field instructor training. Through this model students could begin to appreciate what they have learned and reflect more accurately on what they still need to learn. Field instructors might feel less at odds with the university and more congruent in their practice and field instruction.

References

Bogo, Marion & Vayda, Elaine. (1986). *The practice of field instruction in social work theory and process.* Toronto: University of Toronto Press.

Coady, Nick. (1995). A Reflective/Inductive Model of Practice: Emphasizing Theory-Building for Unique Cases Versus Applying Theory to Practice. In Gayla Rogers (Ed.), *Social work field education: Views and visions.* Dubuque: Kendall/Hunt Publishing Company.

Glaser, Barney G. & Strauss, Anslem L. (1967). *The discovery of grounded theory: Strategies for qualitative research.* New York: Aldine de Gruyter.

Lincoln, Yvonna S. & Guba, Egon G. (1985). *Naturalistic inquiry.* Newbury Park: SAGE Publications, Inc.

Schon, Donald A. (1987). *Educating the reflective practitioner: Toward a new design for teaching and learning in the professions.* San Francisco: Jossey-Bass Publishers.

Schon, Donald A. (1983). *The reflective practitioner, How professionals think in action.* New York: Basic Books, Inc., Publishers.

Chapter 2

Social Work Education
in Health Care Settings:
Using Narrative Approaches

Patrick Clifford

ocial Work in Health Care, published by the Ontario Association of Social Workers, speaks of the presence of social workers wherever health care is delivered (OAPSW, 1986). OASW estimated recently that approximately one third of the social workers in this province practice in the broadly defined area of health care. With the impetus from Dr. Richard Cabot, organizer of the first social service department in the Massachusetts General Hospital in 1905, social work has concerned itself with social, psychological, economic, cultural and environmental factors which contribute to both illness and recovery (OAPSW, 1986). Cabot also perceptively addressed the notion that social workers responded to the feeling states of clients that were often overlooked by those focusing on disease (OAPSW, 1986).

Purpose of Paper

The purpose of this paper is to address the educational requirements of beginning social work professionals in health care settings using post constructionist and narrative approaches in working with clients. There will be a brief examination of the context of social work practice in hospitals during this decade, the traditional skills and knowledge that social workers are expected to acquire and the challenges of newer approaches to work with clients in the health institution. Much of this discussion will draw upon case examples of students' field experience.

Hospital Based Practice

Illness and injury have always had the ability to undermine the usual level of functioning held by the individual. Social workers are often called upon to help in the restoration of equilibrium. The approach has normally been one aimed at assisting the client to regain a sense of order and an improved sense of coping. Social workers in health settings frequently find themselves identifying needs, planning services, supervising and co-ordinating the types of services provided, and offering psychotherapeutic assistance as required (OAPSW, 1986). Social workers do this through the provision of direct and indirect services.

With the evolution of the customer-focused hospital from the hierarchical medically driven institution, social workers are facing even more challenges. Collaboration, co-ordination, sharing and interconnectedness are the new organizational concepts (Globerman & Bogo, 1995). Social workers are being challenged to become generators of knowledge, research oriented, accountable and autonomous. There is an increasing demand that social workers become innovative and change oriented (Globerman & Bogo, 1995). Currently social work students are socialized into the disease-based, mechanistic hospital of the 1990s. They may increasingly be expected to generate research and be accountable, but they are also expected to speak the dominant language of the health institution. This language remains pathology based.

Knowledge Sets for Health Care Practice

To function effectively in the health care institution social workers must acquire two sets of knowledge. The first concerns the language of the institution they work within (i.e. the technical, mechanistic language of health, disease and pathology). The disease model upon which medicine has been built is entirely mechanistic, seeing the body as machine — a machine that periodically breaks down and can be fixed with a pharmacological agent, a surgical procedure, or a therapeutic technique (Weick, 1983). The model depends upon pathology situated within the once-healthy body.

The modern hospital is replete with staff and technology to both diagnose and ameliorate pathology. Hospital-based social workers must be conversant with this language. For example, part of the orientation for social work students includes an overview of the technical language they will require in their work. This knowledge includes disease process, medications and other treatments. Knowledge of diagnostic procedures enables the student to communicate with the rest of the team. Students quickly learn to assimilate broad diagnostic categories with corresponding treatment regimes and with outcomes or prognosis. Diagnosis in the hospital context is the precursor to any form of treatment. It has been suggested that diagnosis provides legitimacy for illness (Weick, 1983). Labels provide meaning. Socially meaningful explanations for particular conditions are conferred in diagnosis and labelling (Weick, 1983).

Clients have come to accept cultural conditioning in which getting better has to do with being told what is wrong by an expert, accepting such teaching, and availing themselves of the prescribed treatment offered by professional healers (Weick, 1983). Students will quickly learn that for an inflammatory arthritis of an aggressive nature, Disease Modifying Arthritic Remitting Drugs (DMARD) will be employed. For a client with a bipolar illness, an antidepressant from the Selective Serotonin Re-uptake Inhibitor (SSRI) family might be employed along with a mood-stabilizing agent. Psychotherapy may be suggested to address the history of trauma behind the depressive state. The student social worker is expected to become proficient with this kind of language. This is not language that is necessarily shared with the patient but rather is used in professional discussions about the patient. A student must learn and adopt this language to participate in team dialogue.

The second set of knowledge students must acquire is related to our own professional knowledge base. Traditionally, social workers have seen their expertise in terms of counselling, psychotherapy, and in a range of indirect services (Cowles & Lefcowitz, 1992). Other professionals have tended to identify social workers with direct instrumental service provision, finding resources, making post-hospital arrangements and so on. In looking at a Bachelor of Social Work curriculum, it was found that students identified a need for increased technical social work skills (such as history taking), more information on disease and pathology (like abnormal psychology), and better preparation for process issues (such as death and dying) to prepare them for work in the health care field (Nutter, Levin & Herbert, 1995). These students also reported they needed better preparation in a variety of therapeutic frames of reference as well, such as solution- and strength-oriented approaches or cognitive behavioural therapy. While educators need to equip students with knowledge, the challenge is in what we teach them this knowledge and its application really means. As we combine the knowledge sets of the institution and profession, we risk a theoretical slide to expert knowledge. As we gain the skills at eliciting from the client his or her story about the disease onset and the impact of the illness on every day life, we become like the physician or the physical therapist before us: the expert with the answers on how to get better.

Social workers become socialized into special theoretical, philosophical, and practice perspectives. We become overly reliant on our favourite intervention theories and inevitably wind up fitting people and their lives into our frame of reference (Gitterman, 1988). It has been suggested that "students need to learn how theory and belief system can sometimes blind us to the ordinary details and actualities of people's lives, their aspirations, anxieties and daily problems" (Gitterman, 1988 p. 36). Weick (1983) speaks of the "giving over" process by the patient as an integral part of the medical model: the client surrenders power and control to the expert knowledge of the physician, to diagnose, treat and prognosticate on the outcome of illness or injury. Within the hospital context, the team has taken on this power, and clients have been well trained to give themselves over to the process if they wish to recover. As we assume professional knowledge and expert opinion on what is wrong with our clients and what they need to do to recover, we invite our clients to surrender to us in that therapeutic journey. This process is often reinforced by the social worker, establishing outside authority as the interpreter of events. As the client allows the social worker to be the guide, the "most fundamental piece of personal power is lost" (Weick, 1983 p. 470).

The expertise of the social worker is not in defining for clients the meaning in their lives, but in relinquishing the worker's power to create contexts of meaning for the clients (Weick, 1983). It is our job as educators to enable emerging professionals to begin to learn how to engage in relationships with clients that are based on our belief in their strengths and abilities. Social work expertise is in helping clients define their own lives and in helping them find or rediscover their own power. Social work practice must assume that people "know what is best for them; this requires a deep respect for people's innate wisdom about themselves and their lives" (Weick, 1983 p. 470). Social workers must help clients re-weave the fabric of meaning in their lives, and the ability to rise to this challenge puts social workers at the heart of the treatment process (Donnelly, 1992).

Narrative and Postmodern Approaches

The notion that no one person, no single theory, and no point of view has privilege at the expense of any other is at the core of postmodernist theory (Parry & Doan, 1994). Postmodernist theories are based on constructionist theories that borrow from literary criticism where "texts are taken apart (deconstructed) and examined for new meaning" (Kelley, 1994 p. 10). Constructionism originates as a school within social psychology where "reality is viewed as constructed in our mind's interaction with (co-constructed) others and with social-cultural forces" (Kelley, 1994 p. 10). What we see and what it means depends on who we are. Kelley (1994) notes that the realities for clients are real; there is real poverty and real violence. But she argues that the power clients give to these realities can be challenged. We can help our clients not to see poverty or illness as intrinsic. We can help them recognize that illness exists, but that they do not have to "be" their illness. For the student learner this may come as a new perspective. The challenge for the field instructor is to work with student learners to come to see clients not as "arthritics" or as "bipolar", but as people with lives and stories that may include an illness.

BSW practicum students, after observing a structured social work interview conducted for a medical rehabilitation program for clients with arthritis, are invited to conduct these interviews themselves. In debriefing consultations after their interviews, students repeatedly reduce clients to a collection of symptoms. Students are good at reporting symptoms and the use of technical language to describe these symptoms. They often find it much more challenging to talk about who the client is. Students will suggest the client is clinically depressed and not functioning. The use of institutional and diagnostic language is apparent. All of the other stories about the client are lost. The fact that the client is in chronic pain, poorly rested and feeling overwhelmed making the journey to the appointment is discounted. The truth of the client becomes the client's illness, and all other facets of their life are lost. As educators of social work professionals we need to equip students to understand that there will not be only one accepted truth.

In the structuralist world of modern mental health care, we are taught to believe that what we see at the surface is derived from what is at the core. The manifestation of depression on the surface is from loss of an object in childhood. The therapist's job is to get at that core, to translate it for the client and to bring about change. Therapy in the postmodernist tradition is not based upon the former insight models, where individuals, troubled with anxiety or depression, come to the therapist to discover themselves, to understand their place in the grand narrative, and to get back on track with integrating into the web. Rather, postmodernist therapy is based on assisting the individual to come to understand the power of the web and the oppressing stories it may tell; the goal is to free the individual to accept or reject stories about the self, based on a more critical evaluation of the array of stories of the self available for belief. For example, a student social worker, after consultation with a client, was able to see that the client believed that because he lost his job and the attendant status that job provided, he was no longer a worthy individual. The client's family had reinforced this perception by indicating he lost his job through negligence and was now lazy and unmotivated to look for work. In addition he had been told and had come to believe that, at a core level, he was afraid of hard work. The depression grew out of his beliefs that he was useless and a coward.

The challenge for the student in this context was to assist the client in evaluating whether he was indeed lazy, or whether there were other versions of the truth about himself that did not fit this picture. The more traditional approach may have been to look for fears at the core of his being, to help him understand what he was afraid of, and to move forward with this new knowledge. The client may have been asked about the usefulness of his symptoms for his life. For the student working with a narrative approach, the client was invited to evaluate whether the concept of production, laziness and cowardliness were the only stories of his life. On a subsequent visit with the client, the student was able to gather an entirely new perspective on this man as she asked questions about those other stories that did not fit with fear and laziness. In between session consultations about the case, the student was encouraged to think about whether the client had been overtaken by the story of laziness. In fact, in audiotape reviews of the sessions, the client would comment on the scope of activities he performed at home now that he "had nothing of value to offer the world." The student would move in to suggest he did indeed have value, and the client would promptly reject the assertion. The student next moved to exploring with him why he had no value. The client was repeatedly invited to relive his pathology.

In becoming open to the stories about the self that have been forgotten or that have failed to have been included in the self description, we must also examine stories that we as social workers and educators may perpetuate that continue to define individuals along the lines of dominant cultural stories. By employing narrative approaches from our consultations, the student social worker, on a subsequent visit, was able to enter into a discussion with the client about the accomplishments around the house and how that did not fit with the dominant story of laziness. An exception to the story of laziness had been found and encouraged further discussions during subsequent sessions.

Diagnosis fails to capture the whole of the person. The danger in diagnosis is in the obscuring of the multiplicity of other stories and dimensions the client carries with him or her. This is not to deny that people have negative experiences. Traumatic experiences such as abuse are real events and need to be acknowledged. However, they are not the sole descriptors of who we are. Problems are not intrinsic to the individual; they are not fixed within persons but rather are shaped by the society and culture persons inhabit. We have long known about the differential classification and prevalence of mental illness across cultural groups. The presence of homosexuality within the Diagnostic and Statistical Manual, and then its absence from those pages, classifies and then declassifies an entire segment of society with pathology.

Another example is the problem with fibromyalgia, a long-term, generalized pain condition with non-restorative sleep and fatigue symptoms. There is some tendency in the health care community to see these clients as difficult to deal with, highly needy and prone to self-absorption in symptoms (Kelley & Clifford, 1997). A student commented that she could not complete an initial assessment in one visit because the client would not stop talking about what hurt. There was some speculation offered by the student about secondary gains. In encouraging the student not to pathologize and to remain curious (a key in narrative work), we explored ways the student could be curious with the client about what she wanted us to understand about her pain. At the next session, the client revealed that she desperately wanted to be believed and had not felt believed in previous interactions with health care providers.

Narrative therapists listen to the stories clients tell. They search with the client for the meaning in the story being told, enquire about the origins of that story, explore the culture and power that reinforce that story, and aid the client in searching for other meanings and other stories forgotten or discarded because they did not fit. Narrative therapists ask questions about power and culture, race and poverty, and gender and science. These broader questions inform the day-to-day existence and meaning for those we see. We need to bring to clients an awareness that anorexia is not their illness. Anorexia is a function of the discourse of western culture, capitalism, patriarchy and gender. The narrative therapist does not situate anorexia in a young female client but rather helps her understand how she has responded to the story anorexia constructs for her.

However, narrative therapy is not about denial of reality; it is not about minimizing the trauma and injustice people face; nor is it about suggesting that all manner of adversity can fade away just by focusing on strengths. In speaking of clients' stories of problems not as intrinsic, but as one story of many, students are encouraged to ask: "How [do] you want to face the experiences you're stuck with" (Cowley & Springen, 1995, p. 74). What kind of relationship do you want with the problem? Narrative approaches emphasize viewing those who consult us as participants in a drama or story, one in which they are able to depart from the script handed to them to give voice to their own words. This departure comes through the process of externalization (White, 1989).

Externalization as a therapeutic concept involves separating problems from persons. Clients who present to us with problems are first helped to deconstruct their stories, to tear them apart and examine them; they are encouraged to examine the roles that society, culture and gender play in maintaining the problem story. In narrative approaches, problems are separated from people to show that individuals may be influenced by a problem (for example, depression or alcoholism), but that they are not composed of or constituted by the problem (Kelley, 1994). This process opens up the way to reclaim themselves from the domination of the problem-saturated story; people are liberated to view problems as external to them and, therefore, in a new light (Parry & Doan, 1994). We may see people who are influenced by, or even dominated by depression, arthritis, or MS, but we are able to view them first as people and then as affected by problems.

BSW students meeting clients for the first time regularly describe the clients they see by the illness they have. Students can outline symptoms of illness, speak about who the client has seen to combat the illness and provide a detailed list of medications. What they often can not do is talk about who the client is, beyond superficial descriptions of mother or husband. Students will often suggest they are overwhelmed by the sheer weight of the physical and emotional burden reported by some of the clients they see.

Case Example

The client, Mrs. M., is a lady in her mid-forties. After having been involved in a work accident, she went on to develop fibromyalgia and what her psychiatrist termed a psychotic depression. When Mrs. M. first came for treatment, she would sit in her chair, rocking back and forth in tears for the better part of the hour. She was frequently not verbal, crying and ringing her hands and saying "I don't know" to questions. She had been this way for three years before referral. This client was completely lost in her story of despair. Her former identity as a self-reliant, hard worker and community figure was lost to one of helplessness. She heard voices that told her she was "no good" and that she should die.

Early on, the work with this woman consisted of discussions of how, since the last visit, she had resisted the voices demanding that she take her own life. She would talk of whether she or the voices she heard were stronger and whether she had ever been strong in her life before. While debriefing after sessions, the student social worker indicated the approach did not fit conventional wisdom. The student asked about ECT and whether the client should be hospitalized or her medications changed. The field instructor began to work to expand the student's understanding of the stories and to encourage her to recognize the incredible strength of the client who stood her ground against the onslaught of symptoms for three years. The work with the client and the student had to do with becoming open to the stories about the self that had been forgotten or that had failed to have been included in the self-description.

As the work progressed with Mrs. M., she cried less and was more and more able to talk about how she had withstood the voices over the last week. The student social worker was able to begin to ask questions about how she was standing up to her death thoughts and eventually her pain. What grew from this work with this particular student was two-fold. She continued to be able to perform an acceptable biopsychosocial assessment, but she also began to display an ability to provide a richer description of clients, beyond a diagnosis and collection of symptoms and factual data. Her growth as a student was in her ability to learn the language of the institution; to gain facility with the interview process; to expand her thinking as an emerging professional to be more curious about the clients' conclusions about their own lives; to engage the clients in some of this curiosity; and, ultimately, to foster growth and change in the clients.

Conclusion

To journey down the road with our clients and to invite them to share with us their stories and experiences, their beliefs and the intimacy of what it all means to them is one of the most fundamental responsibilities of the social work profession. It is a responsibility to be taken with the utmost of seriousness and discharged with the utmost of skill.

We must offer each client the opportunity to examine their stories. As educators it is imperative that we teach those who will succeed us not to simply replay the story our client expects. We must prepare future professionals to broaden the scope, to listen to clients not from the expert's chair, but with curiosity and the most passionate of beliefs in the capacity of those who seek us out to author a new story, should they choose to do so.

References

Cowles, L., & Lefcowitz, M. (1992). Interdisciplinary expectations of the medical social worker in the hospital setting. *Health & Social Work, 17*(1):57-64.

Cowley, G., & Springen, K. (1995). Rewriting life stories. *Newsweek*, April 17, 70-74.

Donnelly, J. (1992). A frame for defining social work in a hospital setting. *Social Work in Health Care, 18*(1):107-119.

Gitterman, A. (1988). Teaching students to connect theory to practice. *Social Work with Groups, 11*(2):33-41.

Globerman, J., & Bogo, M. (1995) Social work and the new integrative hospital. In Gayla Rogers (Ed), *Social work field education: Views and visions*. Kendall/Hunt Dubuque.

Kelley, P. (1994). Integrating systemic and post systemic approaches to social work practice with refugee families. *Families in Society, 75*(9):541-549.

Kelley, P. (1994). The use of narrative work in family therapy. *OAPSW*

Newsmagazine, Autumn 1994,10.

Kelley, P., & Clifford, P. (1997) Coping with chronic pain: Assessing narrative group approaches. *Social Work, 42*(3):266-277

Madigan, S. (1992). The application of Michael Foucault's philosophy in the problem externalizing discourses of Michael White. *Association for Family Therapy, 14*(3):265-281.

Nutter, B., Levin, R., & Herbert, M. (1995). The trend to program management in hospitals: Implications for social work education. In Gayla Rogers (Ed), *Social work field education: Views and visions*. Kendall/Hunt Dubuque.

Ontario Association of Professional Social Workers. (1986). Role of Social Work in Health. Monograph.

Parry, A., & Doan, R. (1994). *Story revisions: Narrative therapy in the postmodern world*. New York. Guilford.

Weick, A. (1983). Issues in overturning a medical model of social work practice. *Social Work*, Nov-Dec:467-471.

White, M. (1989). *The externalizing of the problem and the re-authoring of lives and relationships*. Selected Papers: Michael White. Dulwich Centre Publications. Adelaide. 5-28.

Chapter 3

Program Management in Hospitals and its Implications for the Practice and Teaching of Social Work

Paul Cappuccio

As a social worker who has experienced first hand the evolution of a hospital toward a program management model, I know it can be a frustrating, anxiety-provoking and confusing experience. Although many of the underlying values within program management are shared by the social work profession (autonomy, team work, patient-focused care), in my opinion, the underlying driving force for this organizational change is money. It is important for social workers to understand that the true impetus for change comes from a fiscal restraint perspective. Given, however, that the drive towards a more programmatic hospital will continue as long as hospital budgets continue to shrink, it is also important for the profession of social work, its workers and students, to find meaningful strategies that not only help it survive, but thrive. This is a daunting, and challenging task, given that many workers may be, or already have been, displaced from the health care sector. Yet if we, as social workers, truly believe that patients/clients in hospitals can benefit and become healthier by utilizing social work therapy, then it is incumbent upon us to try to adapt to these new organizational changes, for the betterment of people in need.

This paper provides a brief overview of Program Management — its history, how it has been adapted in the Canadian context, and how it affects the role of social work and the teaching of students. Finally, strategies on how to survive in a changed hospital environment are presented.

Background to Program Management

Program Management is a organizational system that began with Proctor and Gamble in 1928, when they introduced their new product, Lava soap, to the market (Yano-Fung, 1988). Although slow to catch on at first, it eventually became, and still is, the dominant business model. When you look at this model more closely, it makes a great deal of sense. It essentially takes the product, whatever that may be, and makes it the focus of operations. Thus, teams of workers with various skills and responsibilities, under one team leader or manager, work together on producing the product. Instead of having a separate department of engineering, or electronics, each of these service components are brought together to produce a product more efficiently and with greater quality control. The Japanese refined this model even further, by emphasising strong team work and divesting a substantial amount of administrative and managerial control to the "Product Teams."

It appears to make sense on several levels, including fiscally, to have teams of skilled workers, with differing expertise coming together to develop and market a product such as soap, or a car, etc. It was so successful a business model that hospital systems in the United States began to experiment with Program Management as a way of increasing profitability, attempting to control the cost of the medical system, and integrating service delivery. As early as 1973, Johns Hopkins Hospital introduced a management structure that focused on clinical care units as their "products" — anaesthesiology and critical care medicine, gynaecology and obstetrics, laboratory medicine, pediatrics, psychiatry, etc. (Heysell, R., 1985). Each unit became a distinct business entity, with its own budgeting, manager, and internal program planning. Eventually, other hospitals began experimenting with variations of the program management system.

Canadian hospitals began to seriously consider Program Management as an administrative option relatively recently. Many hospitals have moved from a more traditional hospital matrix toward a more programmatic structure, with various modifications and permutations of the Program Management model. It is quickly becoming the expected model of practice for many hospitals. Because this system of operations is based on a profit-oriented paradigm, it has had some interesting results in the publicly funded, not-for-profit settings.

How Does Program Management Work in A Hospital?

To understand why a more programmatic hospital structure is being embraced by hospital administrators, it is important to look at the old hospital structure (see Diagram #1). Most hospitals in Canada worked under a matrix model, or variations of it. Under this model, discreet clinical services such as mental health or surgery were only loosely bound together. Each professional or support worker in the service was accountable to his or her department manager. These departments, such as nursing or social work, had their own budgeting and cost centres. Although a hospital worker may have worked in a certain service, they did not necessarily have to report to anyone in that service. Team work was achieved solely at the clinical level.

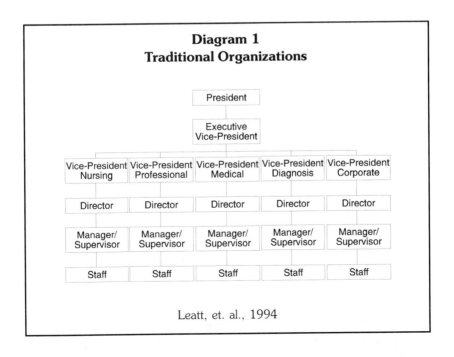

Diagram 1
Traditional Organizations

Leatt, et. al., 1994

Traditional Organizations

For many years, especially when money for the system was in abundance, this model was not problematic enough for administrators to change in a significant way. However, when it became clear that hospital budgets would not be increasing, and, in fact, would be decreasing, hospitals needed a more efficient way of tracking their expenditures. Product line management gave them the opportunity to do just that.

In the United States, the introduction of Diagnosis Related Groups (DRGs) as a mechanism for reimbursing hospitals forced them to consider a product line patient focus. In essence the DRGs are an attempt to objectively track the costs of medical procedures along diagnostic lines (Stuart & Sherrard, 1987). It therefore became important to know how much it cost to perform, for example, the delivery of a baby. Once all the costing could be done, which included everything from physician reimbursement to maintenance and housekeeping costs, a standard could be set, and comparisons between programs and hospitals could be made. Thus began the competition among hospitals for the best bottom line, that is, the lowest DRG costs.

In Canada, a version of the DRGs was developed called the Case Mix Group (CMGs).[1] Once the CMGs were accepted as standard, health ministries began demanding that hospitals find an appropriate way of determining their costing levels for each Case Mix Group. Although this was being done within the traditional hospital model, program management had the ability to track costs more diligently and efficiently and also allocate resources more precisely. It did this by developing cost centres around clinical or diagnostic categories and assigning staff to these centres. Using detailed statistical and workload measurement systems, the hospital could then calculate the precise cost of any procedure. Once the standards were set, it became a race to the bottom line for many hospitals. Success and efficiency for health care began to mean, for governments and administrators, cost containment and, better still, cost reduction.

Practically speaking, Program Management in Canadian hospitals has been successful in eliminating layers of middle management, specifically the elimination of the professional discipline heads. A hospital utilizing Program Management has the ability to streamline its production by the elimination of these reporting layers (see Diagrams #2.1, 2.2, 2.3). Clearly, the reporting lines become simpler, as workers who used to report to their own departments, now report to program managers. This system makes

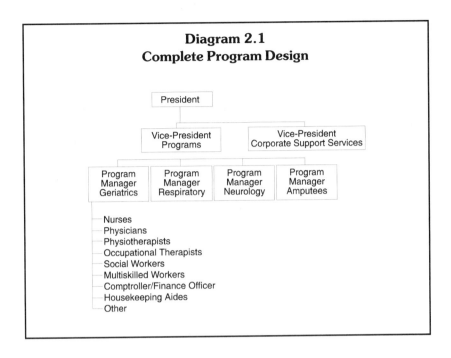

Diagram 2.1
Complete Program Design

President

Vice-President Programs

Vice-President Corporate Support Services

Program Manager Geriatrics

Program Manager Respiratory

Program Manager Neurology

Program Manager Amputees

- Nurses
- Physicians
- Physiotherapists
- Occupational Therapists
- Social Workers
- Multiskilled Workers
- Comptroller/Finance Officer
- Housekeeping Aides
- Other

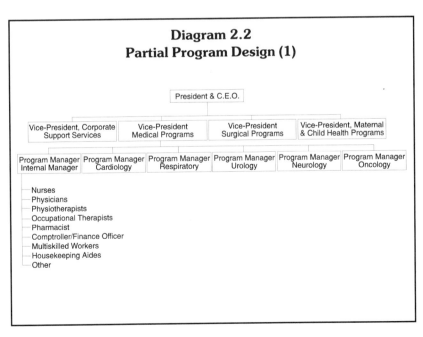

Diagram 2.2
Partial Program Design (1)

President & C.E.O.

Vice-President, Corporate Support Services

Vice-President Medical Programs

Vice-President Surgical Programs

Vice-President, Maternal & Child Health Programs

Program Manager Internal Manager

Program Manager Cardiology

Program Manager Respiratory

Program Manager Urology

Program Manager Neurology

Program Manager Oncology

- Nurses
- Physicians
- Physiotherapists
- Occupational Therapists
- Pharmacist
- Comptroller/Finance Officer
- Multiskilled Workers
- Housekeeping Aides
- Other

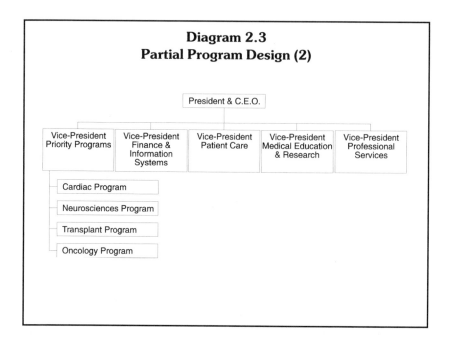

Diagram 2.3
Partial Program Design (2)

managers of most departments redundant, including those of the professional groups such as Social Work, Physiotherapy, Psychology, and Speech Pathology. Each professional, therefore, is assigned to a particular program and reports to a person that, in most cases, is not of their professional background. In this example, there are two managers who are responsible for the running of the programs, an Operations Director and a Physician Director.

In many cases the Operations Director is from the nursing profession, and the Physician Director is obviously a physician. Most professional departments are eliminated, with their budgets and program planning aspects swallowed up by the new Programs. Thus, for example, an Assertiveness Training course that used to be run by the Social Work Department is now run from the Mental Health program. In fact, once Program Management is in place, each program, or discrete business entity has the power to develop, change or eliminate any aspect of programming or professional service. The Managers have the power to review and, if necessary, change or enhance the roles and job descriptions of each professional.

The Role of Social Work Under Program Management

So what does Program Management mean to the profession of Social Work? How does this new management structure effect social workers' day-to-day clinical work? In most instances, I believe, three conditions need to be met for things to run smoothly. Firstly, social workers need to have a strong sense of their profession. Secondly, the workers must have a clear understanding of their role. Thirdly, this role needs to have a broad acceptance by the hospital management. If one or more of these three conditions are unmet, then professional role conflicts can arise. It has been my experience that Program Management inevitably creates tension around role definition.

Program Management demands strong, competent workers who clearly feel confident in their role and have a clear understanding of their functions. "Survival of the fittest" may be a phrase that comes to mind, as social workers struggle to re-examine their role and learn to begin to lobby for their services like they have never done before. The hospital needs to perceive social work as utilizing rational, research-based practice, emphasizing clear outcomes.

In the old hospital system, as powerless as they may have felt at times, social work departments (and in particular Social Work Directors and supervisors) had the responsibility of delineating the roles and functions of the profession, maintaining professional standards, and developing appropriate programs utilizing the specific skills of the profession. Because the role of social worker is often difficult to define and much of what they do owes more to the historical antecedents in their particular organizational culture than it does to any College of Social Work standards, the profession has been particularly vulnerable to role diffusion (ie. the overlapping of duties with other professionals). But even with this dilemma, for the most part, social work departments themselves defined what they did. Other professionals and managers outside of the profession relied on the social workers themselves to tell them what they had to offer the organization.

Because of Program Management and the demise of the social work department (specifically the ending of its budgetary and program planning components, and elimination of the Director), social workers are more vulnerable to direct changes in their professional roles by managers and administrators outside the profession. As anyone who has ever worked in a hospital setting knows, the medical model seems, at times, neither to understand nor value the social work skills of counselling/therapy and advocacy. Unfortunately, to many physicians, social workers are only perceived as valuable when they are expediting patient discharge or disseminating medical information (education or psycho-education). For many social workers in hospitals, it may be the first time that they directly report to a physician (or nurse) and the first time that a physician manager can directly impact on what social workers do, or what they are "supposed" to do.

Not only may physician managers directly affect the role and job description for social workers, but the Program Management model gives these discreet business entities or programs the fiscal power to allocate or reallocate resources. As the money pressures continue to rise in Canadian hospitals, powerful decisions about human resources are being decentralized to the program level, as dictated by the philosophy of Program Management. In and of itself, this decentralization has many potential benefits, as it gives, in theory, the locus of change at the front-line level. However, as fiscal resources diminish, physician managers may be forced to decide that the soft services (ie. non-medical) such as social work may not be worth keeping.

One might argue that the culture for de-valuing social work services in hospitals may have little to do with Program Management and that traditional hospital matrix structures have cultivated the same outcomes. But precisely because of its matrix model, the traditional system gave the social work profession, through its Director, direct access and potential influence to administration. Its voice and, therefore, its philosophy could be heard at management levels that no longer exist in the Program Management structure. As a department, social workers had the ability to cultivate and espouse psychosocial and ecological perspectives. Because many administrators in hospitals were not necessarily physicians, they could be receptive to ideas outside the medical model. Conflicts that arose between professionals, especially those between physicians and others, had administrators in between to mediate. With the new system, social work practice ideas and service delivery could feel pressured to conform to the medical model, given that the workers' direct program manager would most likely be from medicine.

Although not a direct consequence of the Program Management model, the ability to change the functions and roles of a social worker is made easier. Also the political and fiscal climate is established, leading to the de-classifying of the social work position, either by drastic cuts in compensation, or elimination of the profession altogether, replaced with less qualified, lesser paid workers. In my opinion, this scenario is particularly evident in mental health departments where, historically, different professionals overlapped roles. It is not unusual to have Occupational Therapists, Social Workers, Psychologists, and Nurses all running groups or doing counselling. Although each of the professions have aspects of their roles that are distinctive, some of what they do can be performed across all disciplines. When the roles become "generic", it makes perfect fiscal sense to question what type of worker you need and whether the essential work can be performed by someone less qualified and, therefore, less expensive.

It is important to remember that Canadian hospitals are adopting a management model that has, as its chief goals, profitability and efficiency. In private American hospitals, where profitability is the overt goal, the model is seen as effective in achieving this goal. In an article in *Health Care Strategic Management* (1994), George F. Longshore, President and CEO of Longshore + Simmons (a firm specializing in consulting for the health care industry), stated that his studies showed that product line management had the following six "successes":

- occupancy rates were slightly higher (64.6 per cent vs. 63.5 per cent);
- average revenue per beds were higher ($314,000 vs. $262,000);
- average net income per bed were higher ($10,700 vs. $7,603);
- average net income margin was higher (4.5 per cent vs. 3.7 per cent);
- annual admissions per bed were higher (37.1 vs. 34.2); and
- operating profit margin was markedly higher (3.4 per cent vs. 1.6 per cent) (p.15-16).

Stuart & Sherrard (1987), commenting on the success of Program Management at Johns Hopkins Hospital stated: "After more than a decade, the Johns Hopkins experience has been judged a success, from the perspective of its effect on the hospital's financial performance and from that, of achieving an accountable management of services ..." (p. 56). Clearly success here has little to do with things like quality of care, patient satisfaction or clinical outcomes, areas more familiar to social workers. These areas are harder to quantify and easier, therefore, to neglect.

However, some health care providers are expressing concern that a business model may not be appropriate for health care. As early as 1988, Irwin Katz and David Florman, two hospital executives in New York, questioned the use of product-line management in health care. They worried that profitable services such as in-vitro fertilization may be offered at the expense of less profitable services such as AIDS treatment. Florman stated that a hospital's mission, which includes community service, may, at times, supersede strict adherence to product-line management (Solovy, 1989). The May 9, 1996 edition of the *Globe and Mail*, in an article entitled "Business theory seen as failure in hospital," examined the work of Professor Pat Armstrong and Professor Jerry White. After surveying employees from 10 hospitals, their study questioned the efficacy and portability of business practices in health care. They were also concerned about the paucity of examination being done on whether "production-management techniques" were suited to the hospital environment (Globe & Mail, May 9, 1996). There is, however, still very little qualitative literature in this area.

Challenges for Educating Students

The challenge of educating Social Work Students within Program Management is clear. Although the process of teaching may be untouched by the new administrative structure, the changing role of the social worker in the hospital setting itself sets up troubling dynamics. If the role of the social worker becomes more generic and less centred around traditional social work roles, the supervising worker may feel caught in a teaching dilemma: does the worker teach the student the traditional roles and values, thereby continuing the tradition of the importance of psycho-social assessments, counselling skills, and advocacy, or does the worker teach the student about the "job," which may entail roles the profession is not used to emphasizing, such as education, recreational and socialization work, and strict "paperwork" discharge planning (that is, filling out forms without working through the psychological and social aspects with clients and families). By teaching the student the "job," it may better prepare them for future employment. Yet if we, as professionals, succumb to external pressures and change our roles, are we beginning to internalize the new roles and values? Are we beginning to redefine our role to conform to the hospitals', or other professionals' expectations?

Students are particularly vulnerable to the changing environment of hospital work. Historically, field work and academia have always had inherent tensions that challenged students and forced them to synthesize the two experiences into the formation of their own theoretical practice framework. If successful, field practice challenged students to forge social work theory into practice. But for this to be successful, the field instructor needed to feel comfortable that the work and theory could blend. If the field instructor thinks that the work has changed to an extent that social work teaching becomes incongruent with the work place environment, the instructor is caught in a dilemma.

As an example, let us imagine that counselling is no longer a social work function in a hospital and that psychosocial assessments of family dynamics, psychological processes and social functioning have been replaced by practical discharge planning protocols aimed at expediting discharge. How can students learn the essential clinical skills of assessment and intervention, when those skills are not only considered unimportant to the job, but may also be seen as a hinderance in doing the job efficiently? The practical field instructor may decide that, for the student's future, it may be best to de-emphasize the clinical skills and teach the student "the ropes," so to speak.

Let us look at another example. Social workers in mental health may be asked to teach clients about their illnesses, using a biological model that may explicitly state that psychological or social factors play little to no role in the etiology of mental illness. Since a physician is likely the manager in the Program Management model, the instructors, for their own survival, may have no choice but to teach this philosophy. How do field instructors teach their students, at the same time, the ecological perspective, or other social work theories? Again practical instructors may tire of the struggle, and simply teach students the "job."

Some Strategies

I strongly believe social workers must not abandon the struggle to protect and enhance the unique nature of hospital social work practice: in particular, the role of psychosocial assessments, counselling/therapy and advocacy. The strength of our profession lies in the roots of these core functions. By diminishing them, we begin to internalize the expectations of others outside the profession who view social work as a quasi-profession and perhaps expendable. As difficult as it may be, the insistence of professional standards of practice and the enhancement of clinical skills is the only way to ensure that students continue to espouse social work perspectives. It may eventually lead to the displacement of hospital social workers, but if we slowly change our roles away from our strengths and teaching institutions begin to lessen their demands, then it may be inevitable that what made us a unique discipline in health may disappear.

There are, however, more positive strategies that social workers can adopt to ensure its survival. Judith Globerman and Marion Bogo (1995) suggest that the development and implementation of a Social Work Professional Standards Group would help maintain educational, research and teaching standards. Although not a new concept, it challenges social workers to maintain and, indeed, to enhance their practice by providing a organizational vehicle, namely the Professional Practice Group, in which workers support and develop each other's professional growth.

A strong presence from the Social Work schools in hospitals will also help maintain high standards. By setting teaching and field curriculum standards, the schools have an obligation not only to understand the new hospital structures but to come up with strategies for field instruction, to help them in teaching students within the new environment. The schools must demand that the profession continue to provide students in hospitals with high-quality placement experiences, even though there may be pressures by hospitals to set lower standards.

Also, some of the core values of Program Management are shared with the profession of social work. By building on the shared values of team empowerment, autonomy, organizational negotiations and mediation, and change adaptation, social workers can be seen as a leading force in the organization. By reminding the organization that there are non-fiscal benefits to be derived from the change and that these need to be focused on as well, social workers can be perceived as attempting to build bridges within the new organization.

Endnote

1   A statistical tool used in Canadian hospitals, first developed in the 1980s, and modelled after the U.S. DRG's (diagnosis related groups), to "compare output among hospitals." It classifies patients diagnostically and has the ability to discern the average cost of treating these patients. Thus, length of

stay benchmarks can be developed and compared in and among hospitals. The four criteria for CMGs are: "the patient groups have to make clinical sense, they have to be based on routinely collected data, there has to be a manageable number of groups and they have to be statistically homogeneous with respect to length of stay in hospital." (All quotes taken from Pink, George et al, "Physicians in health care management; 3. Case Mix Groups and Resource Intensity Weights: An overview for physicians", *Canadian Medical Association Journal.* 1994; 150(6).)

References

Coutts, J. (1996). Business theory seen as failure in hospitals. *Globe & Mail,* (May 9, 1996).

Globerman, J. & Bogo, M. (1995). Social work and the new integrative hospital. *Social Work in Health Care, 21*(3):1-21.

Heysell, R. et al. (1985). Decentralized management in a teaching hospital. *New England Journal of Medicine, 310* (February): 53-56.

Leatt, P., Lemeiux-Charles, L., & Aird, C.(Eds.).(1994). *Program management and beyond: Management innovations in Ontario hospitals.* Ottawa: Canadian College of Health Services Executives.

Longshore, G.F. (1994) Hospitals look to a new breed of product line managers to lead them into the future. *Health Care Strategic Management* (November): 15-19.

Ontario Association of Professional Social Workers (February, 1993). OAPSW Discussion paper on program management in health care settings.

Pink, George et al, Physicians in health care management; 3. Case mix groups and resource intensity weights: An overview for physicians. *Canadian Medical Association Journal.* 1994; 150(6).

Solovy, A. (1989). Limited use for product management in hospitals. *Hospitals* (January 20, 72).

Stuart, N., & Sherrard, H. (1987). Managing hospitals from a program management perspective. *Health Management Forum, 8*(1): 53-63.

Yano-Fong, D.(1988). Advantages and disadvantages of product-line management. *Nursing Management, 19*(5): 27-32.

SECTION II

APPROACHES TO FIELD EDUCATION DELIVERY

Chapter 4

Documentation as a Teaching Tool

Gayla Rogers
Barbara Thomlison

The ultimate goal of professional social work education is the competent application of core skills and theory to a variety of practice situations encountered by incumbent professionals. The practicum is designed to assist learners in achieving the necessary skills, attitudes, and application of knowledge. It provides the opportunity to teach social work students competencies for practice through both direct case practice and indirect processes such as documenting practice. Documentation is a supportive tool which teaches students about practice, practice decisions, and the development of a professional self. The act of writing about an experience opens the mind for reflection and analysis and is the precursor for integration and synthesis, which is the desired outcome of quality learning. This type of learning does not happen automatically, nor is the transfer of knowledge content into practice a spontaneous process. Different methods of documenting practice will meet the needs of students with diverse learning experiences and learning styles.

The Outcomes of Practicum Learning

The bridge between theory and practice is, to some extent, a function of instructional design. The partnership between academy and the practicum should produce students who learn to challenge themselves critically in practice situations with new and different questions. Students need to master not only content knowledge, but also self-knowledge, reasoning and decision-making skills for effective interventions. These are necessary components for ongoing learning. Therefore, it is important to identify the instructional designs and tools to best assist students in learning to think critically. As well, there are tools to promote and assist students in taking responsibility for their learning. Documentation tools are designed to help students in their efforts to strive for clarity, precision, accuracy, and depth and breadth of learning in the practicum. Understanding the learning styles of social work students is a necessary part of identifying teaching strategies and is a key component in determining which documentation tools to use.

Documentation as a Teaching Tool

Documentation as a teaching tool in an agency setting serves different purposes. Some types of documents serve to articulate students' learning goals. Other types of recording meet the service requirements of the setting by documenting the social work process. Therefore documenting practice involves administrative tasks such as recording information in certain preplanned ways according to agency convention. This kind of documentation typically relates what went on when a student provided service (content), describes how the student handled a session (process), and how the student understands the issues or problems facing the client system (context). At a more complex level, documenting practice involves educative tasks such as analysis, integration, synthesis and critical self-reflection. Therefore, knowledge in the use of both process recordings and videotaped recordings, the two most common forms of documentation, is essential to the enhancement of student learning in the practicum.

The process recording is almost as old as social work. They are written accounts of interviews made after they have taken place. They are useful because they can include the students' feelings and interpretations, which may not be the same thing at all as what the client thinks took place or what actually did take place. It provides students with the opportunity to recall and reflect on any feelings they experienced during an interview. These feelings can then be reviewed and their possible effect on the client can be assessed. By providing an approximate text of the interview, the process recording allows the practicum instructor to follow the interview, see the steps that were taken, the skills that were used, and provide the student with useful feedback.

Through a videotaped recording, students can sort out the facts from their feelings and their hypotheses or speculations about the client's thoughts and feelings. Students can reflect on the process, as well as the content of the interview. They can consider what they know, along with what they sense about clients and their situations. Students' reflections are an important source of data about decisions, but direct access to students' work via a videotaped recording allows the practicum instructor to see the actual practice. In this way the practicum instructor may see problems or strengths that students may not have identified.

Both methods of documentation provide the student and practicum instructor with different information about the student's learning. As well, knowing about a student's preferred approach to learning helps the practicum instructor make better supervisory choices.

Study Purpose

The following section presents one aspect of a larger study to enhance field-based learning (Rogers & Thomlison, 1996). The study explores the preferred learning styles of undergraduate social work students and its influence on their use of and preference for documentation tools to facilitate learning in the practicum.

Assessing Learning Styles

The Gregorc Style Delineator (Gregorc, 1982, 1984) is a reliable and valid instrument that determines a student's preferred learning across two dimensions with four possible categories: concrete sequential, abstract sequential, abstract random, and concrete random. Briefly, concrete sequential persons are product-oriented, practical, more structured, ordered and objective. Abstract sequential persons are rational, evaluative, and logical. Abstract random persons are person-oriented, sensitive, realistic, and spontaneous. Concrete random persons are risk-takers, flexible, concerned with multi-solutions, and responsive to perceptive approaches to learning.

Phases of the Study

This exploratory study consisted of several phases. First, a curriculum was developed to include a set of exercises that were designed to match field-based tasks, activities, and processes for student and faculty-field liaison use in the practicum and integrative seminar. Second, to ensure consistent implementation of the curriculum among faculty-field liaisons, a faculty development process was constructed. Third, an assessment of social work student learning styles was arranged through the University of Calgary Teaching Development Office. Finally, a questionnaire was designed to capture student experiences with the set of exercises.

In the Fall semester of 1995, the entire fourth-year undergraduate social work population who were about to enter their first practicum were invited to participate in this field-based learning project. Practicum time consisted of three days per week for 24 hours per week over a 15 week semester. Students were organized into six sections where approximately 14 students met for an integrative field seminar throughout the term. The six faculty members who assumed responsibility for the integrative field seminar were also responsible for the faculty-field liaison .

During the practicum orientation of the Fall 1995 term, the Gregorc Style Delineator was group administered to the students by the director of the University's Teaching Development Office, who was highly experienced with the measure and the procedures. Based on this procedure all student learning styles were determined and recorded. Students then completed the set of exercises throughout the practicum. After the completion of each exercise, students were required to complete a questionnaire assessing the effectiveness of the exercise to the students' learning; these questionaires were collected by the faculty-field liaison and returned to the researchers.

The Documentation Exercises

Exercises were developed based on the recognition that students have different learning approaches. Students were required to complete three different assignments representing three approaches to documenting practice assignments. The three documentation exercises asked students to:

(1) analyze a selected segment of an interview (Exercise M.1);
(2) provide a narrative reflection of practice (Exercise M.2), and
(3) analyze a whole interview (Exercise F.1).

The first two exercises on documentation (M.1 and M.2) were required at mid-term and the last exercise (F.1) was required at the end of the practicum (see Appendix for exercises M.1, M.2, and F.1).

Upon completion of the documentation tasks, students completed a questionnaire assessing each of the exercises. This questionnaire was structured as a likert-type scale. The form contained 15 items asking students to evaluate the recently completed exercise (either M.1, M.2, or F.1). The form used item scores that ranged from 1 = strongly disagree to 5 = strongly agree. Some of the items were positively worded statements and others were negatively worded to partially control for response set bias. Higher scores represented stronger positive responses to the exercise and lower scores indicated negative or less positive responses to the exercise.

Findings

Participant Characteristics

Of the 84 fourth-year eligible social work students, 79 (94 per cent) individuals volunteered to participate in the study. Of these, 65 (82.3 per cent) were female. The participants' mean age was 30.4 years, and 13 (17.4 per cent) were aged 40 years or older. The majority reported being Caucasian (69 or 87.3 per cent), and none reported the presence of a disability. As a group, participants were experienced academically, but inexperienced professionally. Fifty (63.3 per cent) of the 79 students had a bachelor's degree and 17 students (21.5 per cent) entered with a college diploma. One student had a master's degree. The mean years of professional social work experience reported by participants was 1.84 years (S.D. = 3.6). Over half of participants reported having no previous social work experience (41 or 51.9 per cent), while 8 participants (10.1 per cent) had five or more years of previous professional experience.

Learning Styles

A total of 77 (97.5 per cent) volunteer students completed the Gregorc Mind Style Delineator. On this instrument scores can range from 0 to 40. Scores of 27 to 40 are considered to represent a dominant learning style. Table 1 shows that the single largest dominant learning style for these students was abstract random (AR). Thirty-two students (41.6 per cent) displayed an AR dominant learning style, as indicated by their highest score for any learning style. Over half of the students (49 or 63.6 per cent) may be considered AR dominant by virtue of obtaining a score of 27 or higher for that learning style. This is possible because individuals may be dominant (scores over 27) in more than one learning style.

Table 1
Gregorc Mind Style Delineator Scores and Dominant Styles (N=77)

	Concrete Sequential (CS)	Abstract Sequential (AS)	Abstract Random (AR)	Concrete Random (CR)
Mean Score	25.24	22.22	27.40	25.20
S.D.	(5.7)	(4.2)	(5.1)	(5.5)
Number of students dominant in style, as measured by #1 style	24 (31.2%)	5 (6.5%)	32 (41.6%)	15 (19.5%)
Number of students dominant in style, as measured by a score of 27 or higher*	35 (45.5%)	11 (14.3%)	49 (63.6%)	27 (35.1%)

* One student showed no dominant learning style, as indicated by a score of 27 or higher on any one dimension of the Mind Style Delineator.

The data, however, show a split in the dominant learning styles of the students. The second most common dominant learning style among the students was concrete sequential (CS). Twenty-four (31.2 per cent) of the class displayed a preference for this learning style, as indicated by their highest score on the Mind Style Delineator. A total of 35 students (45.5 per cent) showed a CS dominance for at least one of their dominant learning styles. These are students who prefer learning that is linked to concrete, physical senses, progressing in a linear step-by-step fashion, and a clearly defined final product. Finally, one other group of concrete learners exists within this cohort — the concrete random (CR) learners. Fifteen participants

(19.5 per cent) achieved a higher score on the CR dimension of the Mind Style Delineator than for any other learning style.

These figures become important when one examines the clusters formed by the learning styles. The pattern of learning styles shows two significant clusters within a class of social work students. The single largest or predominant learning style among these students is the abstract random or AR learning style. At the same time, there is a significant cluster of individuals, the CS learners, whose optimal learning may occur in ways directly opposite to one those of AR learners. This suggests a wide range of student understanding and paths to learning within this cohort and difficult challenges for course design and instruction. The fact that concrete learners (CS and CR students together) constitute 50.7% of this BSW population makes the distinction between concrete and abstract learning even stronger.

When examining those students who displayed more than one dominant learning style, a number of interesting combinations emerged. Twenty-one students (27.2 per cent) were dominant for both AR and CR learning styles, meaning that they were random learners who could adapt to both concrete and abstract learning situations. Five more students (6.5 per cent) were dominant for both CS and AS learning styles. Such students could be expected to prefer sequential learning situations, of either concrete or abstract form. Three students (3.9 per cent) were dominant for both CS and CR learning styles, and would likely learn well in either sequential or random ways, but would prefer concrete subject matter and examples. Finally, one student (1.3 per cent) was dominant for AS and AR learning styles. This student was primarily an abstract learner, but one who could easily learn in both sequential and random fashion.

Analysis of the Documentation Exercises

Table 2 shows a Summary of Student Mean Ratings and Targeted Learning Style for the three documentation exercises. Ratings for these exercises were positive as indicated by mean rating scores that varied from 65.4 to 60.1. These ratings, however, cannot be considered indicative of strongly positive attitudes toward the structured exercises. Rather, they may represent widely varying opinions about the usefulness and effectiveness of the exercises. Evidence of this can be found in the widely differing maximum and minimum rating scores for each exercise, for example, 98.3 for exercise F.1 to 16.7 for exercise M.2, and the resulting large standard deviations found for ratings of each exercise. Such variation in the ratings of exercises was, in fact, anticipated as it was expected that students with different learning styles would rate exercises geared toward their learning style more favourably.

Table 2
Student Ratings of Structured Learning Exercises
(N=77)

Exercise	Topic	Targeted Learning Style	Mean Rating	S.D.	Max.
M.1	Analyzing a segment interview	CS	65.4	19.4	93.3
M.2	Narrative reflections on practice	AR	60.1	21.9	95.0
F. 1	Analysing a whole interview	CS & AR	63.8	22.9	98.3

Further analyses sought to detect statistically significant differences in the mean ratings of the documentation exercises by students' dominant learning styles. In particular, analyses targeted differences between concrete-sequential (CS) and abstract-random dominant students, as the exercises were conceptualized as appealing to one of these two groups. To test for these differences, analysis of variance (ANOVA) analyses were done for each exercise. Results indicated, however, that no statistically significant differences existed between mean ratings of the exercises by any of the four dominant learning styles. That is, even though some differences in the mean ratings for exercises do exist on the basis of dominant learning styles, these differences are not large enough to be considered significant.

In examining differences in the mean ratings of all the exercises, however, it was noted that the ratings sometimes appeared to differ along the lines of one learning dimension. This dimension could be concrete dominant students (CS and CR), abstract dominant students (AS and AR), sequential dominant students (CS and AS), or random dominant students (AS and AR). T-test analyses were therefore conducted to determine if significant differences in ratings of the exercises existed between concrete versus abstract dominant students and sequential versus random dominant students.

The only statistically significant finding was that concrete dominant students rated Exercise M.2 significantly higher than abstract dominant students (t = 2.35, df=27, p = .027). Concrete dominant students' mean rating for this exercise was 69.44, as compared to the abstract dominant students' mean rating of 51.90. Again, this result is surprising, given that Exercise M.2 was conceptualized as an abstract random exercise, one that asked students to tell their story by describing an account and writing a narrative of a recent encounter in practice.

Individual results for each of the exercises are discussed as follows:

Exercise M.1 Results

M.1 is an exercise entitled "Analyzing a Selected Segment." The purpose of the exercise is to provide students with a tool for a detailed analysis of a segment of their practice. Students are asked to recall the dialogues for a segment of an interview session and then to do a detailed analysis of that segment following a format provided. This exercise is prepared for a concrete sequential (CS) learning style students.

Students generally appear to have found Exercise M.1. useful. This is supported by the means of Item 6 (4.03), Item 13 (3.88), Item 9 (3.55), and Item 2 (3.51). Together the means on these items suggest that the students found the exercise increased their understanding and knowledge and was both relevant and applicable to social work practice.

Table 3 below shows that concrete dominant students (CS and CR) rated the exercise higher than abstract students. Contrary to our expectations, however, ratings by CS dominant students were not higher at a statistically significant level.

Table 3
Summary of Dominant Learning Style for Exercise M.1

Dominant Learning Style	N	Mean	S.D.	Median
CS	8	70.62	19.51	75.8
AS	1	N/A	N/A	N/A
AR	11	58.48	19.5	55
CR	4	73.75	7.12	71.6

Exercise M.2 Results

Exercise M.2 is called "Narrative Reflection of Practice." The purpose of the exercise is to understand the meaning of a particular intervention. Students were asked to tell their story by describing an account and writing a narrative or a chronicle of a recent encounter in practice. They were also asked to reflect upon the meaning this piece of practice had for them and those with whom they were involved. A taped recording of the practice encounter was also required. This exercise is prepared for students with "abstract-random" (AR) learning styles.

Students were not as favourable toward Exercise M.2 as they were towards Exercise M.1. The exercise was not considered as clear (Item 1 mean of 3.57), as likely to increase understanding of the topic (Item 2 mean of 3.26), or to make students more knowledgeable about the topic (Item 5 mean of 3.06). Nor were students strongly in support of recommending this exercise to other students. This is evidenced by the mean response of 2.94 to Item 15.

The data below (Table 4) show that some students were more positive toward Exercise M.2 than others. Surprisingly, it was not the AR students this exercise was designed for who most favoured the exercise (mean of 53.71). Rather, it was concrete dominant students (CS and CR) who showed the highest ratings for the exercise. These differences, however, were not statistically significant.

Table 4
Summary of Dominant Learning Style for Exercise M.2

Dominant Learning Style	N	Mean	S.D.	Median
CS	11	69.09	19.87	66.66
AS	1	N/A	N/A	N/A
AR	13	53.71	22.06	50
CR	4	70.41	13.35	72.5

Exercise F.1 Results

Exercise F.1 is called "Analyzing the Whole Interview." The purpose of the exercise is to provide students with a tool for reflecting on their practice. Students are asked to reflect on a whole interview session. Specifically, in analyzing the interview as a whole, they are required to identify the purpose of the interview, to describe the interview, and to present the content of the interview. This exercise is prepared for both concrete-sequential (CS) and abstract-random (AR) learning style students.

It should be noted that only 14 students completed Exercise F.1. This makes interpretation of means difficult. It is interesting to note, however, that these students thought the exercise was applicable to social work practice (Item 6 mean of 4.05). They were not as positive, though, about whether the exercise was relevant to their learning (Item 6 mean of 3.63) or whether it made them more knowledgeable about the topic (Item 5 mean of 3.15).

Due to the low numbers of students who completed Exercise F.1, it is impossible to detect statistically significant differences between groups of students. However, of the AR students who completed the exercise, they did not rate the exercise as positively as other students, as shown in Table 5 below.

Table 5
Summary of Dominant Learning Style for Exercise F.1

Dominant Learning Style	N	Mean	S.D.	Median
CS	3	66.11	36.37	73.33
AS	1	N/A	N/A	N/A
AR	5	59.66	23.25	61.06
CR	3	71.66	6.66	71.66

Summary Discussion

Student comments about each of the exercises also provide further understanding to the learning with each of the exercises. Qualitative comments from students about Exercise M.1 (Analyzing a Selected Segment of Practice) express typical positive features as follows:

- Although enlightening and worthwhile, this exercise required a lot of time outside the practicum.
- This exercise adds stress for me because it is not graded; you do some assignments to jump through hoops.

- There is nothing negative about this exercise.
- The exercise provides opportunity for me to think back and consider for myself the aspects of the intervention.
- This exercise is more beneficial than a process recording.

Few negative student comments were reported but the following responses indicate learning challenges from the student:

- The exercise is time consuming.
- It is difficult to analyze interventions in community settings; specific interventions do not unfold in a practice encounter.
- It is difficult to describe the details of an intervention.

For Exercise M.2 (Narrative Reflection of Practice), many more comments were reported. The most positive features according to the students indicate:

- This makes one think about interventions and effectiveness.
- This gave me an opportunity to write about a particular learning opportunity I had and then to share this essay with my supervisor. We had a chance to discuss points in my written essay.
- Being asked the meaning of the essay was a positive experience.
- I knew it was important for my personal growth but this exercise did not give me any new insights.
- It made me think about the impact of an intervention and hopefully look at both the anticipated as well as unanticipated consequences.
- Reporting the details of the intervention is difficult but helpful.
- Reflection on my interviewing styles was enlightening.
- This exercise was not too structured. It made me utilize my writing skills.
- Reflecting on what you do and what it means to you is a key element in understanding yourself and how you might practice.
- It provides the opportuntity to think back and consider for yourself the aspects of the intervention, so that through reflection you can learn how to better undertake practice in the future.
- I could hear how an interview went and then could reflect how things could be done differently.
- This is more beneficial than a process recording.

This exercise also generated the most negative qualitative comments from students. Although students expressed the comments as negative features of an exercise, in some cases the comments indicate the degree a student's learning was extended. The following comments are indicative of issues of concern:

- Some of these exercises are not that easy to do.
- For me, this particular exercise was not a positive experience. It was a duplication of what I am required to do on an assessment/ intervention interview. My supervisor and I discuss practice at all levels I encounter and, it is also thoroughly documented in each and every file I work on.
- It was a repetitious and time consuming exercise.
- It felt like I was analyzing to death.
- My interviewing is very directional in correction.
- I did not understand the purpose of the exercise.
- It was describing the details of the interventions.
- Nothing is negative (a view shared by many students about this exercise).
- This exercise is difficult to do.
- Taped recordings should not be required; it is difficult to connect to theory at the same time as doing practice.
- I am frustrated trying to fit myself into this.
- Community interventions do not unfold in one practice encounter.

For the final documentation Exercise F.1 (Analyzing the Whole Interview), the following positive features were reported:

- This exercise is useful to do as an ongoing basis to be aware of what skills we are using and what we need to be reminded of.
- The verbatim part of the exercise is very helpful; it made me realize that I should pay attention to "exactly" what the person says.
- This exercise is very easy to understand.
- Although one may feel one is doing well (and one may be), one can still always learn from others looking at the same situation.
- It forced me to take a hard, analytical look at my interviewing skills (or lack of).

The most negative features of Exercise F.1 (Analyzing the Whole Interview) were summed up by the following few remarks:

- This exercise has no relevance to community work and makes no sense to me.
- It is difficult to write everything out word for word.
- This exercise is time consuming.
- My practicum does not see clients in direct contact, only in a group.

In summary, it appears that documentation assignments in the practicum serve as learning tools and as evidence of what students accomplish. Different methods of documenting practice serve different purposes and, as well, facilitate differential learning depending on students' learning styles. Therefore, it is essential for social work programs and, specifically, the practicum to offer learning choices and a range of methods by which students can analyze their work. It does, however, require social work field educators to take time to identify students' preferred learning approaches and design opportunities to assist students in active learning for a wide range of practice experiences and settings.

Students who show preference for the concrete learning styles prefer good organization skills, a focus on detail, brainstorming, and they like to know how things work. They will have difficulty with abstract interpretations and difficulty in being imaginative. Concrete learners like to start with examples first and then the theory. The student who shows preference for the abstract learning styles researchs information, analyzes and interprets ideas, works well with others, and displays sensitivity to the feelings of others. Challenges include difficulty in organizing and in providing exact answers or details. These students learn by viewing the concepts and theory first, followed by specific examples.

In this study, social work students show dominance for the abstract random learning style, closely followed by the concrete sequential approach to learning. This suggests social work students prefer deductive learning, starting with broad concepts and theories and then working on examples in an attempt to link with their perceptions and intuition. The findings indicate that practical and theoretical learning is a highly complex and individualized process requiring further study. Learning about the ways to assist students in this process is, of course, not simple. Social work programs should be encouraged to offer training and support for practicum educators to understand the preferred learning approaches of students and the variety of methods to assist students with documentation for learning. Both students and practicum instructors can potentially benefit from discovering their preferred learning processes. Furthermore, students need to be encouraged to broaden and stretch themselves and extend their repertoire of learning strategies, thereby enriching the field-based curriculum and learning experience.

References

Gregorc, A. (1982). *Gregorc style delineator: Development, technical and administrative manual.* Maynard, MA: Gabriel Systems.

Gregorc, A. (1984). Style as a symptom: A phenomenological perspective. *Theory into Practice, 23* (1):51-55.

Rogers, G. & Thomlison, B. (1996). *Learning styles and structured exercises: Enhancing field-based learning.* Final research report for The University of Calgary, Teaching.

APPENDIX I

Exercise M.1

Name: _____

I.D.: _____

Analyzing a Selected Segment

Purpose: To provide you with a tool for a detailed analysis of a segment of your practice.

Exercise: Analyzing a segment of an interview will help you link the process and the skills with the phase of practice and give you an opportunity to consider alternatives. Immediately following an interview, attempt to recall the dialogue for a segment of the session that you would like to subject to detailed analysis. Use the form provided.

✓ Column 1: Verbatim account: This should be close to total recall of what was said in the interview. It should include both you and your interviewee's statements.

✓ Column 2: Your feelings: This column allows you to identify what you were feeling at the time the verbal exchange was taking place. This column is for you to link your feelings with your actions.

✓ Column 3: Communication skill: This column allows you to label or identify the specific communication skill(s) you are using.

✓ Column 4: Phase: This column identifies the phase of the interview, such as, engaging, contracting, middle phase, work phase, or termination phase.

✓ Column 5: Alternative statements: The column provides a space where you can propose an alternative response. If you had it to do over again what might you have preferred to say. This column will help you consider what you could have done differently.

✓ Column 6: Field instructor's comments: This column is for your field instructor to make notes and provide feedback to you.

APPENDIX II

Exercise M.2

Name: _____

I.D.: _____

Narrative Reflection of Practice

Purpose: To understand the meaning of a particular practice intervention.

Exercise: Tell your story by describing an account and writing a narrative or a chronicle of a recent encounter in practice. In addition to reporting the details of the intervention that unfolded, reflect upon the meaning this piece of practice had for you and those with whom you were involved. Hand in a taped recording of the practice encounter along with your narrative reflection of practice.

APPENDIX III

Exercise F.1

Name: _____

I.D.: _____

Analyzing the Whole Interview

Purpose: To provide you with a tool for reflecting on your practice.

Exercise: It is important to critically reflect on your practice. Making a structure to do this will enable you to note your skills, strengths and areas needing improvement. Immediately following an interview or after listening to the tape of an interview, reflect on the whole session using the directions on the following page.

In analyzing the interview as a whole:

✓ Identify the purpose of the interview: You should be directed toward formulating a statement of purpose that is concise, clear, and specific in relation to the proposed interview. It should show the relatedness between this interview and any previous work and should also reflect your awareness of the particular function of your field placement.

✓ Describe the interview: You should record your general impressions of the physical and emotional climate at the outset of the interview and, more specifically, its impact on your interviewee.

✓ Present the content of the interview: This part of the record should be devoted to the actual description of the interaction during the interview. However, this should not be a verbatim account but a *selective* review of the salient issues, themes, and topics. The length of this section of your recording depends on your stage of development and learning patterns. It should at the very least include:

- A description of how the interview began.
- Pertinent factual information.
- A discussion of the process of the interview, how it unfolded, and the influences on the part of both you and your interviewee had on impacting the outcome.
- Link theory and knowledge to practice. You should identify the source of experience you drew upon to inform the decisions that were taken during the interview. This process gradually develops into conceptual thinking as you begin to integrate course content and theoretical material with your practice skills in an actual interview.
- Reflect on practice. You should reflect on the content and process of your interview in relation to its purpose and final outcome. This includes identifying your strengths and weaknesses in the interview and some directions for your future work.

Chapter 5

A Student Seminar Program: An Innovative Complementary Educational Program in the Field

Nona Moscovitz
Helen Szewello Allen

The field placement experience has a profound influence on a social work student's professional development. The field experience offers students practical educational opportunities, allowing for the integration of their knowledge and the development of competent practice skills. For students entering into a new field placement, the experience is often overwhelming. In retrospect, my first field placement experience sixteen years ago was marked by feelings of insecurity, inadequacy, and isolation as I took on a new role in an unfamiliar work setting. Over the years I have observed that entering a totally new environment is a difficult and stressful experience for many students. The feelings of stress associated with beginning a new placement may impact on their adjustment and impede their capacity to learn.

It is, therefore, important for field placement settings to acknowledge and understand the challenges students face when they enter the field and address the various concerns that may interfere with their ability to learn. This paper will describe and evaluate a student seminar program designed to facilitate student entry and management of their field experience. As well, it will demonstrate how a student seminar program can mediate students' feelings of isolation, help them integrate into the field, and provide the necessary supports while addressing their learning needs. This paper will also argue that such a complementary agency-based educational program can be a vital catalyst for field placements in an agency context where a significant number of students are placed at the same time.

Theoretical Framework

Entering a field placement, while anticipated with great enthusiasm by social work students eager to practice, necessitates a major shift in roles. The familiar and secure environment of the classroom is replaced by a complex agency structure, with skilled practitioners carrying out varieties of tasks, initially appearing unfamiliar to a student. Further, anticipation about the expectations to work with "real" clients and to be supervised through a one-to-one close relationship with a field instructor, adds to the complexity of relationships and assignments that a student will have to manage in their new learning environment. It is thus understandable that beginning a new field placement can result in confusion and feelings of being overwhelmed (Nisivoccia, 1990). Intimidation and self-doubt are often inherent in a student's field placement experience at the onset. Rompf, Royse and Dhooper (1993) have also suggested that attempts to establish relationships with new field instructors and staff as they adapt to a new environment with unfamiliar agency procedures is a real challenge for students. For students to successfully establish themselves and have a positive learning experience in the field, a review of the literature suggests four areas that need to be addressed: the environment, integration, peer support and learning needs. The following diagram illustrates these inter-connected concepts that are vital to consider when planning for successful field placements for students and illustrates how a student seminar program connects these components.

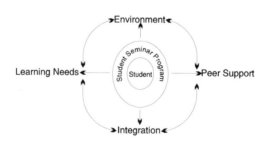

The Environment

It is essential that a field placement provide a safe, non-threatening milieu for student learning. Research has shown (Kaplan, 1988; Rompf, Rose & Dhooper, 1993) that students report high levels of anxiety related to the field placement experience. The students' fear of authority and/or their anticipation of the field instructor's expectations of competent performance in the field can result in feelings of inadequacy. Students often enter the field perceiving themselves as lacking in knowledge and skill. Having to prove their ability in the chosen profession can be a tremendous source of anxiety (Grossman, Jordano, Shearer, 1990). Further, Kaplan (1988) has established that high anxiety levels interfere with complex types of learning, particularly of tasks that are unfamiliar and/or dependent on the acquisition of new skills rather than depending on former knowledge and experience.

Aware of the psychological stresses of the beginning students, the staff of the receiving agency must carefully plan the students' initial entry into the field placements. Because the exploratory study of social work students by Rompf, Rose and Dhooper (1993) found that the students demonstrated high levels of anxiety as they prepared to enter the practicum, they suggested that receiving agencies should provide formal orientation programs for incoming students. Unfortunately, they do not elaborate on what components would be necessary in such a program to help the students reduce their levels of anxiety and stress.

Drawing from his years of study and knowledge of adult education methods, Knowles (1971) states that the student's learning environment sets the backdrop for all learning, and he suggests that the creation of a nurturing atmosphere is critical to a student's educational success. The agency environment needs to be comfortable, informal, flexible, open and trusting. Moscovitz (1995) demonstrated that the kind of orientation provided to the students as they enter into a new learning environment will have an impact on the quality of their relationships with the field setting and, ultimately, on the achievement of their learning goals and ability to provide appropriate social services to clients.

Learning Needs

In today's rapidly evolving and turbulent world, the landscape of social work becomes more complex and challenging. New social problems are emerging, social service cutbacks are placing additional pressure on busy practitioners, while new practice partnerships are being forged in the push for inter-disciplinary integration. Students, now more than ever, need to be better prepared for the complexities of the practice milieu and the demands for professional autonomy and leadership. Various approaches have been suggested to prepare students for the emerging challenges of practice. Henry (1975) advocates for an urgent need to expose students to a variety of populations, settings and types of services within the student's field placement experience. He offers alternative practicum experiences for students by introducing a model of field instruction comprised of five agencies. Referred to as the Field Instruction Centre, this structure encourages a diverse learning experience as students have the opportunity to engage in different service delivery systems. Further supporting the need for diverse learning experiences, Kaplan (1988) reports that students are concerned that their exposure is limited when working on only one or two projects or too few cases and recommends that students be exposed to a wider range of practice issues. Bogo and Globerman (1995) argue that a well-structured educational experience in the practicum, in close partnership with the university's educational goals, allows the students to broaden their view of social work practice. While the traditional method of field instruction, the one-to-one relationship, continues to be vital for the student's learning process, this can be complemented by additional structured learning opportunities. Adding additional instructional components can complement individual field instruction, and can also provide an effective means of exposing students to a wider range of practice situations and knowledge about social problems than that provided by their individual assignments. There is evidence to suggest that student seminars are complementary to individual field instruction and can play a significant role in a student's academic learning (Henry, 1975). Through mutual exchange, students expand their learning as they hear about other students' experiences from different departments and/or settings. This, in turn, maximizes their motivation when listening to many challenging cases. It provides a "forum for interactive learning, and mutual exchange in field instruction principles and practices" (Rogers & McDonald, 1992, p. 163). Viewed as a continuum of learning, links are made between academia and the field placement setting in the student seminars. These links give the students the opportunity to link specific knowledge gained from the seminars to their own clientele.

Further, additional information can be provided on special topics that is helpful for all students to have, information that the individual field instructor may not have the time or expertise to provide.

Integration/Peer Support

Student seminars can provide students with a sense of belonging and an enhanced sense of group cohesiveness: they are all in the same boat as equals. By meeting other students and becoming familiar with their new setting, students are no longer so anxious and are able to focus on their roles and expectations (Gitterman, 1989). Within a common setting, students experiencing new situations look to one another for security, reassurance and comfort (Kaplan, 1988). How students view one another and exchange information have a significant impact on their field experience. A peer support group establishes an atmosphere that reduces the students' sense of isolation and offers them emotional support that, in turn, results in a more enriched field experience. As Cassel (1976) describes, this happens as a result of new and strengthened relationships in a more adequate social network. As noted in group work literature, when individuals find a place to discuss their mutual problems and how they deal with them, as well as a place to share common worries and interests, they begin to feel validated and reassured by their group (Robinson, 1979; Gitterman, 1989; Kurtz & Powell, 1987; Shulman, 1982; Marshack & Glassman, 1991). A positive element inherent in peer relations is the sense of security that can develop. This helps to reduce isolation and lessen anxiety when insecurities arise in situations of integrating into new surroundings, allowing for a focus on expectations of learning new methods for problem solving and reflective analysis of social problems and practice responses. Cohesiveness is thus fostered in peer group settings because of a common experience and a shared sense of unfamiliarity (Compher, Myers, Mauro, 1994). While student seminars provide an organized forum for interactive learning and mutual exchange, they also can create a support group atmosphere, allowing students to understand that their own initial practice mistakes and difficulties are not the result of their own particular shortcomings but a shared experience and part of the learning process (Kadushin, 1976). This results in reduced levels of stress and improves the individual's capacity to learn and develop competence.

Kurtz and Powell (1987) highlight social relationships, social learning and cognitive changes as the three components that contribute to the effectiveness of self-help groups. Although they refer to self-help groups primarily in reference to clients, this concept of mutual aid can be adapted in a working environment with students to foster an atmosphere of sharing and allow them the opportunity to express and work on emotional and practical concerns related to their field placement experience in a safe, non-threatening milieu. As pointed out by Kadushin (1976), "The group not only provides the opportunity for lateral teaching — peer-to-peer — but provides opportunities of mutual aid of various kinds" (p. 324). It helps them to express and identify issues or conflicts intrinsic to their learning, such as feeling inadequate, fearful, overwhelmed, and concerned with professionalism and student/supervisor issues (Bogo & Vayda, 1987). Through a formal, organized and structured educational experience that fosters mutual interdependence, students offer each other reciprocity, encouragement, and consolation (Moscovitz, 1996). Through mutual exchange, the students expand their learning as they hear about other students' experiences from other departments and/or settings, broaden their knowledge of new areas of practice, and gain a place for analysis and reflection, all of which helps them to link theory and practice.

In summary, it is evident that the staff at a field placement need to appreciate and understand where the students are at when they arrive to begin their field placement experience. Attending to the environmental climate, integration into the setting and beginning practice, receiving and giving peer support and meeting learning needs can be ameliorated through a group process in a student seminar program. The following example of how one agency accomplished this will provide us with a model that could be utilized by various agencies.

Background to the Development of an Educational Program

The CLSC René-Cassin/University Institute of Social Gerontology is a local community health and social service centre in Montreal, Quebec, providing services to a territory that has a high concentration of seniors (60+). In addition, this CLSC is designated as a University Institute of Social

Gerontology, which is closely affiliated with the three major universities in Quebec: McGill, Université de Montréal, and Université du Quebec à Montréal. This status provides the CLSC René-Cassin with the mandate to become a centre of excellence in the area of social gerontology, including research, services, and programming. This designation also carries with it a commitment to provide training to students from various levels (community colleges, undergraduate, graduate, post-graduate) and from various disciplines and specialities. Recognized as a progressive and innovative teaching facility, the CLSC René-Cassin believes in the professional development of its students and staff (Policies and Procedures, CLSC Rene-Cassin, 1996).

On April 1st, 1993, a massive reorganization of social services in Quebec occurred when Bill 120 was passed. At the CLSC René-Cassin, the number of professional staff grew from 26 to 46 persons. With this increase in professionals came the increased demand from educational institutions and diverse disciplines for field placement opportunities for students.

In September 1993, twelve students entered the CLSC René-Cassin, an agency experiencing transition and growth. New staff were slowly integrating into the structure and personnel were being reorganized at the CLSC. This restructuring further complicated staff cohesion by creating two agency work sites (within 8 km of each other) to accommodate the increased staff.

As a result of the many structural changes, a student seminar program was conceptualized, developed and implemented at the CLSC René-Cassin to bring together all the students who were doing their field placement in various departments at the CLSC. It was felt that by collectively meeting on a regular basis, the students' sense of "belonging" in a large and fluid establishment would be enhanced as they became oriented and integrated into the CLSC René-Cassin. This paper will describe and analyze the impact this program has had on both the agency and staff of the CLSC René-Cassin as it embarked on a new approach to teaching students within the field placement experience. In the program's third year, the CLSC René-Cassin had over fifty students from diverse disciplines and academic settings in the field placement (Moscovitz, 1996).

The following table illustrates the breakdown of student placements by teaching establishment and profession in the third year of the program.

Breakdown of Student Placement
by Teaching Establishment and Profession
September 1995 - September 1996

Discipline	McGill	U de M	UQAM	Concordia	Ottawa	Pierre Mendes-France	John Abbott	Vanier	Marie Victorin	Dawson	PSBGM Riverside Tech Centre
Social Work U1	3										
U2	5										
U3	3	2	2		1						
Special BSW	1										
MSW	3	1			1	1					
Nursing	4	2									
Physiotherapy	1										
Occupational Therapy	6	1									
Recreation Therapy				4							
Special Care								3			
Social Services									2	2	
Dental Hygiene							2				
Homecare											2
Community, Recreation & Leadership Training										2	

TOTAL NUMBER OF STUDENTS: 54

Description of the Student Seminar Program

The agency designated an Educational Co-ordinator who would be responsible for co-ordinating, planning, and animating all seminars, lectures and tours for the Student Seminar Program, as well as any field instructor meetings. Also, acting as ombudsperson, the Educational Co-ordinator offered field instructor's feedback from issues raised by students and provided consultation with field instructors and students in relation to problems in the field and within the agency. The Educational Co-ordinator provided an environment that was non-threatening and non-evaluative to both students and field instructors in order to ensure increased openness and participation. All the students were told about this service at orientation day, and they were encouraged to approach the Educational Co-ordinator at any time should problems arise in the field. This problem-solving process has proven beneficial to all parties involved.

The program consists of two well-developed and structured units. Each September, the influx of students marks the end of summer and ushers in the beginning of another academic year. The Student Seminar Program welcomes the incoming students by organizing an orientation day, which is generally the first day of field placement for most students. This first day offers a first-hand overview of the structure and policies of the field placement setting to students from various disciplines and numerous teaching establishments. The importance of this day is recognized by the field instructors and students alike. A comprehensive information package consisting of updated, relevant material on the agency and its territory is distributed to all students along with an identification card. A tour is arranged to help orient the students to the physical environment. The orientation day introduces the students to the field placement setting and sets the climate for the year to come. Knowles (1971) emphasizes the need to establish the climate of the field setting and states that it is important that a formal entry level orientation be provided to all students beginning a field placement.

As well, Student Seminars are offered bi-monthly and are open to all students at the agency. The variety of disciplines represented in the student group poses a challenge to the Educational Co-ordinator when planning the seminars. Content of the seminars cannot be oriented to specific professions and specific skill development is not emphasized. The challenge lies in programming seminars that are generic in nature and relevant to the multi-disciplined student population present (Moscovitz, 1996). The diversity within the group encourages the notion of multi-disciplinarity that already exists within this agency. The different perceptions and orientations of the students, even those within the same profession but from different universities, stimulate exchange and debate.

By bringing students together, the seminars provide them with the opportunity to expand their learning as they hear about other students' experiences from other disciplines or departments. As well, they provide a forum for exchange in thought and orientation with a group composite of multi-disciplinary students and staff, which further reflects the character and philosophy of the agency. They expose students to a wider range of practice situations than that provided by their individual assignments and give students the opportunity to link specific knowledge gained from the seminars to their own clientele. By using diverse teaching methods in the seminars, such as role playing, videotapes and writing workshops, the staff encourage the students to make links between theory and practice.

Within this seminar model, the students use the forum for active group participation in analyzing, discussing and linking concepts to real situations facing the student and/or the establishment. This structured teaching program provides seminars on issues related to policy and practice within the agency, visits to community resources, in-house lectures by staff in their area of expertise (eg: elder abuse, conjugal violence, multi-cultural issues), writing workshops, and case presentations. It is an effective way for teaching the broader perspective of social work practice. The opportunity for greater exposure to well qualified and specialized staff at the agency who present at the seminars benefits the students and staff, "Not only do students learn from each other, but the supervisor learns from teaching different students, things that will be of value to all" (Pettes, 1967, p. 97). Thus, this structure allows for exposure to additional role models in addition to the students' individual field instructors. The seminars that include the writing workshops have a direct impact on the quality and uniformity of the students' work at the agency and provide an additional support to the field instructors by reducing the amount of time spent reviewing agency forms. The following table is an outline of a recent schedule of the Student Seminar Program.

A second component to the Student Seminar Program is the field instructors' meetings, which are held three times during the year. These meetings provide an opportunity to exchange supervisory ideas and concerns, which, in turn, leads to a sense of peer support. Having been given the opportunity to participate in such a forum, the field instructors

Student Seminar Program		
Date	Program	
September	Orientation Day	
September	Seminar:	The first interview - Do's and Don'ts
		Confidentiality and Ethical Issues
October	Writing Workshop:	Bio-Psycho-social Evaluations
October	Tour:	Montreal Holocaust Memorial Centre
October	Lecture:	Alzheimer's
November	Tour:	Maimonides Hospital - Chronic Care/Long Term Placement - Foster Home Unit
November	Writing Workshop:	Psycho-social Reporting
November	Seminar:	Multicultural Issues
January	Seminar:	Conjugal Violence
January	Writing Workshop:	"CTMSP" (public placement application)
February	Presentation:	from AMI-Quebec (Association for the Mentally Ill)
March	Seminar:	Elder Abuse
April	Closing Luncheon	

have clearly identified where their agency needs to further develop in the area of field education. The opportunity for exchange and dialogue empowers the practitioners, which provides the impetus to take control of their own professional education.

One of the outcomes of the field instructors' meetings, recognized as vital in the continued excellence as a teaching establishment, was the field instructors' request for further training and skill development. The concerns raised and expressed by field instructors and students through oral and written feedback supported the perception that field instructor training should be emphasized, encouraged and promoted (Moscovitz, 1995). The field instructors believed that their agency was responsible for the development of their professional competence and plans for training were undertaken by the Department of Professional Services.

The objectives for a training program were divided into three "phases." Firstly, a training program was offered to all past and present field instructors in the hopes of establishing training and skill development that encouraged uniformity, consistency and a professionalism in supervisory practices with students.

Secondly, a field education model was developed that helped establish criteria for future field instructors and students (Moscovitz, 1996). The task of developing a field education model that would reflect the agency's philosophy, teaching program and learning opportunities was undertaken by a core group of field instructors at the agency. This model has a methodological framework that provides a foundation for field instruction practice. It also provides criteria for future field instructors, teaching establishments and students wishing to participate in the field placement experience. This undertaking further reflected this group's commitment, expertise and partnership in field education within this agency. It is the agency's vision, once this Field Education Model is completed, to offer in-house training to new and less seasoned field instructors by a staff person who has had previous field instructor experience, has participated in the Field Instructors' Training and has been identified as a "trainer."

Thirdly, the agency, by offering a structured educational program also enhanced its partnership with academic institutions. This commitment supported the work of the teaching establishments by reinforcing and contributing to the student's development of knowledge. With the existence of the Student Seminar Program, field instructors had become more critical of their own needs as a teaching centre vis-à-vis the role of field liaisons from teaching establishments. As they moved towards clearer field instructor role definitions and practice modalities, they recognized what external supports were needed to provide the highest level of field education to the students. As a result, the agency was able to place greater demands on some teaching establishments to have the university field liaison play a more active role within the field placement setting.

The Student Seminar Program has become recognized by other academic institutions as a progressive and well-developed program. This, in turn, has attracted students from many teaching establishments within and beyond Montreal. As well, other field placement settings have expressed an interest in the program and have requested consultation to help them set up such a program.

Evaluation

At the end of the third year of the program, a student and field instructor evaluation was developed and implemented to measure the effectiveness of the Student Seminar Program. This evaluation process for both students and field instructors allowed for more input into the future planning of the program.

During the third year of the Student Seminar Program, a Student Questionnaire was distributed to all CLSC Renè-Cassin students (n=19) (Moscovitz, 1996). In general, the majority of the students were satisfied with their experience at the CLSC René-Cassin, which supported their verbal feedback throughout the year. They rated their level of learning as excellent (85 per cent) and the field placement itself was considered "very good" to "excellent" by most students (92 per cent). All the students (100 per cent) responded that the Student Seminar Program made a "great" to "very great" difference and that it enhanced their field experience at the CLSC René-Cassin.

Throughout the third year of the program, verbal feedback received from students was recorded. As well, interviews were conducted with two students at the end of their field placement. Several themes emerged that reinforced and supported the theoretical framework of this program. Students' first impressions were strongly influenced by the orientation day organized by the agency. A valuable discovery gleaned from student's oral feedback, questionnaire and interviews was the tremendous impact the orientation day had. It had not only introduced the students to the agency but set the climate for the year to come. As expressed by one student, the importance of being made to feel comfortable by the warm reception offered had a direct impact on her initial anticipatory concerns of entering a new setting: "The first day of field placement felt very good. I thought the reception was excellent, that the students were not an aside, that we were given a certain importance as students and that was very nice." This experience supports the assertion by Rompf, Rose and Dhooper's (1993) recommendation that the development of a formal orientation program to reduce student anxiety is vital. The orientation day at the agency provided the venue for students to feel a fundamental part of the field placement setting which helped to reduce their levels of anxiety. It is therefore strongly recommended that a formal entry level orientation be provided to all students beginning a field placement because it reduces their anxiety levels and makes them feel supported and valued in their role as a student.

As stated earlier, Kaplan (1988) and Henry (1975) emphasized the importance of exposing students to a wider range of practice issues. One student stated that, "There are a lot of resources to learn about the things that I needed to learn. The Student Seminar Program brought me knowledge from the seminars." Complementing this comment was the 92 per cent of students who responded in the questionnaire that they felt that the Student Seminar Program made a "great" to "very great" difference in the variety of practice issues they were exposed to. As one student commented: "As students, we don't have a tremendous amount of experience. The more exposure we can have ... the better. All this is provided and is very beneficial in the program." Looked upon as a continuum of learning, the link is made between academia and the field placement setting through the Student Seminar Program. To another student, the program "filled the gaps that I wasn't getting at school and that was excellent. It gave me information regarding certain things that I had not been able to take because of scheduling, time and course load."

The group seminars provided a mechanism to deal with issues and concerns in the field. Acknowledging the benefits of participating in a group experience (Compher, Meyers & Mauro, 1994), one student felt that the setting encouraged peer support, group cohesiveness and allowed for mutual exchange: "It brought more cohesiveness among the students ... more of a rapport between us."

One of the most interesting themes that emerged was that the most dependable friendships were formed by those students who shared a common office. It had originally been believed and advocated by the Educational Co-ordinator that providing students with individual space to work in was important. The development of interpersonal relationships for those students sharing office space was reported as most significant and satisfying. Offering a forum for problem solving and reciprocity, many of the students' offices became self-supporting, interdependent settings. This outcome has influenced how student office space is planned in the future.

As expressed by many students, a clearly defined educational program specifically designed for students was an integral factor to their integration and adjustment into a large structure with 100 per cent of student respondents indicating that the program provided something extra that was not offered at other field placements.

At the same time a Field Instructor Questionnaire was distributed to all CLSC René-Cassin field instructors (Moscovitz, 1996). The questionnaire was divided into three sections, asking field instructors their opinions about their experience regarding agency supports, teaching establishment supports and professional satisfaction. The majority of field instructors (79 per cent) responded that the CLSC was quite helpful in providing "in-house" field instruction training. This reinforced the positive verbal feedback previously received regarding the field instructor training offered in the previous year. One field instructor commented that there is a "need for regular meetings of field instructors for support and sharing of models and techniques." Eighty-four percent indicated that the agency was quite helpful in organizing a student orientation at the beginning of the field placement and supplemental training to students throughout the year. The orientation of students was one of the top three most important agency supports. However, 84 per cent reported that the agency was not particularly helpful with regards to their caseload. As one field instructor wrote: "The greatest impediment to being a field instructor is the weight of my caseload which has never been reduced." However, it was also very rewarding to find that the majority of respondents (89 per cent) reported that they derived enjoyment from their role as a field instructor and felt that they were contributing to their profession.

Field instructors were not as happy about the teaching establishments' supports. Eighty-four per cent felt that they had little opportunity to influence the teaching establishments' curriculum and that feedback from these establishments was lacking. These comments have been passed on to educational institutions at various meetings. As a result, the Educational Co-ordinator was invited by one of the universities to sit on their Field Development Committee for one year, and she was able to provide ongoing feedback on field instruction issues and student learning needs from her experience with the Student Seminar Program.

Conclusion

This paper has described a Student Seminar Program that offers students a richer and broader source of learning while providing excellence in the educational experience for both students and staff. The Student Seminar Program at the CLSC René-Cassin has become a vital part of the student's field placement experience and an integral part of the agency.

After three years, the continuing evolution of the Student Seminar Program has enhanced the profile of the CLSC René-Cassin as a teaching facility. The program continues to surpass the initial expectations. Having the capacity to become leaders in training and the transfer of knowledge to students is reflected in the agency's interest in educational seminars. Denoting the importance of field education at the CLSC René-Cassin, one of the agency's annual objectives is to promote field education and its field instructors.

This program encourages new approaches to teaching in the field that allows the student the increased capacity to learn within a more nurturing and secure setting. Student integration and adjustment, peer support and a broader range of learning can be achieved by offering a structured educational program in the field. Field placements need to begin organizing more formal structured programs in order to respond to the incoming students' anxieties and concerns. The Student Seminar Program has paved the way for the growth of new ideas and directions as it has inspired the movement towards further program development in previously uncharted waters. It has made an important contribution to knowledge building in the area of field education. While the program is a good one, it too faces the challenges of ongoing cutbacks, reallocation of funding and staff, and serious time constraints. A creative educational program versus direct service delivery to the agency's clientele is a difficult choice to make and may create a conflict between management and field instructors in reaching a decision. Evidently, there is great disparity from one agency to another on how these issues are being addressed. Some have developed programs, others have not. Reasons may vary from lack of resources, insufficient time or lack of interest. However, given the changing realities of agency and school practices, an educational program in the field can ensure that the school and field educators are meeting a common goal: preparing students for the challenges they will face as professionals during very uncertain times.

References

Abels, P. (1970). On the nature of supervision: The medium is the group, in Munson, C. (ed.). (1979). *Social work supervision.* New York: The Free Press. (133-142).

Abels, P. (1978). Group supervision of students and staff, in Kaslow, F. (ed.). (1978). *Supervision, consultation and staff training in the helping professions.* San Francisco: Jossey-Bass. (176).

Bogo, M. & Globerman, J. (1995). Creating effective university-field partnerships: An analysis of two inter-organization models for field education. *Journal of Teaching in Social Work, 11*(1/2):177-191.

Castile, J. (1976). The contribution of the social environment to host resistance. *American Journal of Epidemiology, 104*:107-123.

CLSC René-Cassin\University Institute of Social Gerontology of Quebec. (1996). *Interviews with social work students.*

CLSC René-Cassin\University Institute of Social Gerontology of Quebec. (1996). *Policy and procedures on field placements.*

Compher, J. V.; Meyers, R. & Mauro, L. (1994). Agency-based student support groups and the relationship between field instructors and student: Essential learning modes in public welfare. *Field instruction in social work settings.* by T. Schwaber Kerson (ed.). (1994). New York: Haworth Press. (3-90).

Gitterman, A. (1989). Building mutual supports in groups. *Social Work With Groups, 12*(2):5-21. Haworth Press.

Grossman, B.; Levine-Jordan, N. & Shearer, P. (1990). Working with students' emotional reactions in the field: An educational framework. *The Clinical Supervisor, 8*(1): 23-39. Haworth Press.

Henry, C. St. George. (Fall, 1975). An examination of fieldwork models at Adelphi University School of Social Work. *Journal of Education for Social Work, 11*(3):62-68.

Kadushin, A. (1976). *Supervision in social work.* New York: Columbian University Press.

Kaplan, T. (1988). Group field instruction: rationale and practical application *Social Work With Groups, 11*(1/2):125-143.

Kaplan, T. (1991). A model for group supervision for social work: Implications for the profession, in *Field education in social work: Contemporary issues and trends,* (141-148), by D. Schneck, B. Grossman, U. Glassman (eds.). Dubuque, Iowa: Kendall/Hunt Publishing.

Knowles, M.S. (January 1971). Innovations in teaching styles and approaches based upon adult learning. *Education for Social Work,* (32-39).

Kurtz, L.F. & Powell, T.J. (Fall, 1987). Three approaches to understanding self-help groups. *Social Work with Groups, 10*(3):69-78. Haworth Press.

Marshack, E. & Glassman, U. (1991). Innovative models for field instruction: Departing from traditional methods. *Contemporary Issues and Trends*, (84-95), by D. Schneck, B. Grossman, U. Glassman (eds.). Dubuque, Iowa: Kendall/Hunt Publishing.

Moscovitz, N. (1995). *Summary document of the student seminar program.* Unpublished document at the CLSC René-Cassin.

Moscovitz, N. (1996). *Summary document of the student seminar program.* Unpublished document at the CLSC René-Cassin.

Moscovitz, N. (1996). *Student seminar in the field.* Unpublished paper presented at the Social Work Field Education Conference, June 1996.

Nisivoccia, D. (1990). Teaching and learning tasks in the beginning phase of field instruction. *The Clinical Supervisor, 8*(1):7-21. Haworth Press.

Pettes, D. (1967). *Supervision in social work.* London: George Allen & Unwin.

Rompf, E.L.; Rose, D. & Dhooper, S.S. (1993). Anxiety preceding field work: What students worry about. *Journal of Teaching in Social Work, 7*(2):81-95. Haworth Press.

Robinson, D. & Robinson, F. (1979). *A guide to self-help groups: From self-help to health.* London: Concord Books.

Rogers, G. & McDonald, L. (1992). Thinking critically: An approach to field instructor training. *Journal of Social Work Education, 28*(2):166-177.

Shulman, L. (1979). *The skills of helping individuals and groups.* Illinois: Peacock.

Vayda, E. & Bogo, M. (1987). *The practice of field instruction in social work.* Toronto: University of Toronto Press.

Chapter 6

A Group Supervision Program

Jeanne Michaud

We live in a time of restraint. It is true in Ontario, Quebec and all over Canada. Government response to large public deficits is to revise the "welfare state" we have experienced in the last several decades. This has had an impact on the organization and distribution of health and social services. A strong wind of "neo-liberalism" blows all over the country with consequences on social work education. We must think of new ways to prepare students to cope with different problems occurring in different systems. We must also elaborate strategies to provide training by which students will be equipped to face the pressure of services with more requests and less resources.

In work settings, those social workers interested in field instruction have developed a group supervision program which complements individual supervision for student training. This paper aims to describe the context in which the objectives of the program have been developed. It will also outline the structure and content of a group supervision experience in a time of restraint when field instructors are attempting to work within fiscal limitations and prepare their students for functioning under a lot of pressure without becoming burned out.

Context and History

The Group Supervision Program is offered to students from Laval and/or Sherbrooke University in their second or third year of studies for their Bachelor degree in Social Work (B.S.W.).

During their University education, students have two placements with a field instructor in a public institution or community organization. Each placement has a duration of eleven to fifteen weeks and is an integrated part of the Bachelor program. I work in the Young Offenders Service of Quebec Youth Center. I am a field instructor for five to six students at one time. Some of my colleagues also work with students doing their placement. We form a group which varies from seven to ten students with two to four instructors.

I will explain briefly the structure and organization of our services. In Quebec, the Young Offenders Services are the responsibility of the Director of Youth Protection (D.Y.P.). The Provincial Director is the same person as the Director of Youth Protection, and there are as many (D.Y.P.s) as there are administrative regions in the province (sixteen). There are also two or three other regions in the northern part of Quebec with special agreements with Native Indians.

Quebec Youth Center is a public institution which includes Youth Protection Services, Young Offender Services, Adoption Services, Foster Care, Rehabilitation and Detention Services for youth and children. From a legal perspective, it is a structure quite similar to a public hospital. Moreover, the revised Provincial Health and Social Services Act creates University Institutes in the health and social services fields. These Institutes promote research and teaching in the field.

A year ago, the Quebec Youth Center received the status of University Institute affiliation with Laval University. The population targeted are children, youth and their families who experience severe adaptation and integration difficulties.

The Group Supervision Program was first introduced in 1985 by a group of field instructors working for Young Offenders Services. I became the co-ordinator of that program in 1990. With time, the program has evolved to the present state I am outlining in this report.

Objectives

The placements have five objectives, which derive from the five steps of the intervention process. These are: analysis of the situation, identification of the targeted-problem, plan of action, execution of action and evaluation of action. In addition, we also would like the students to experience the helping relationship, where they have the responsibility of a number of youth cases (between 5 to 12). They act as youth workers for youngsters with a probation order. They also evaluate situations where alternative measures can be proposed and they may have to present a pre-disposition report in Court. All these tasks are monitored by a field instructor.

The Group Supervision Program in our service complements individual supervision. It was developed with four major considerations in mind. Firstly, we want to give the students the opportunity to observe different ways of intervention through work with different clients and different workers. This provides a richness through a larger variety of situations and gives more opportunity for experimentation. Secondly, we would like to create an atmosphere of mutual support. The use of authority and intervention with non-voluntary clients imposes a heavy emotional burden, and it is important to develop mutual support among a team of social workers. Thirdly, working with a group also means saving time for the instructor. He or she gives information about the organization etc., which does not have to be repeated. Finally, the instructors find it beneficial when they can share their observations about the students. It is a way to develop a more objective view and a way to compare perspectives of the students' progress, even though the evaluation remains the individual responsibility of the instructor.

Program: Content and Structure

The content of the program includes four major themes:

1. Practical application of theories of delinquency and social work intervention.
2. Knowledge about the setting, the context (specifically Young Offenders Act, etc.) and the partners (Justice, Rehabilitation Centers and Community organizations, etc.).
3. Development of self awareness (values, boundaries, transference and counter-transference, etc.).
4. Enhancement of abilities required to fulfill tasks (pre-disposition report, criteria of evaluation, etc.).

The themes are developed during orientation week and weekly meetings. During the first week students are in the setting, a field instructor introduces them to the institution, the Quebec Youth Center. He presents the structure, the services and their physical location, as well as a brief explanation of when and how to use them. The presentation includes a video and a visit to the main building. He also introduces them to other colleagues. The day ends with the sharing of individual expectations. On the first day we aim to create a warm atmosphere by doing an "icebreaker." The students choose a partner and introduce one another and then present their partner to the group. The second day focuses mostly on the Young Offenders Act. We make a brief presentation of the different steps in the judiciary process and highlight our role by illustrating how we fulfill the mandate of a youth worker. This includes a visit to the Juvenile Court and meetings with the different partners there. These partners include a Crown attorney, a judge, a defence attorney, a clerk and a police officer. We also visit some parts of the Court building.

At another time during the week, the students visit a Detention Center where a child care worker explains the various programs offered and how everyday life is organized. The group meets again with one of the instructors for a presentation of a client file. This is an exploration of the content of a client file and how to access information within the file. Students are then given free time to settle themselves in their office.

The week ends with a meeting of all the instructors and the students who are involved in the Group Supervision Program for the semester. This activity concentrates on creating links in the group and developing self-awareness in relationship with others. For example, we often use a game to reach these objectives. We call it the "Perceptions Game" (Simon, P. & Albert, L. 1975). Everybody sits in a circle. We ask everyone, including the instructors, to choose four people in the group, regardless of sex or age who represent,for them, the image of a father, a mother, a brother or sister, and a friend. Everyone takes ten to twenty minutes to make their choices. Following this, each student reveals their choices and gives short explanations of these choices. Those students selected give their feedback on the choice made. The goal of this activity is to assist students to develop a greater awareness of how different people (clients or workers) can react differently when responding to the same person, and how they may also project different images to different people. This type of exercise creates a better understanding and rapport in the group and is done with mutual respect, even though we know that it provokes various emotions. At this time in the placement, the members of the group are not very familiar with one another. Therefore, they tend to express positive rather than negative attributes about each other. The experiment of talking about one another is easily accepted and agreeable. One aspect that could be more difficult to accept is the fact that sometimes there are students who are rarely or never chosen. This situation and emotional reactions can be discussed because the choices that are made are based on first impressions. Moreover, the field instructors believe that students in placement should be able to deal with this. These reactions can also be discussed in individual supervision.

After the first week, the group meets a total of 10 to 12 times (nearly once a week) for two-and-a-half to three hours each time. In these meetings, we suggest different exercises. Three of these exercises are:

1. Decision game (this game was developed by J.Trépanier École, de criminologie, Université de Montréal).
   Participants have to make suggestions to the Court about a teenager who pleaded guilty to a criminal charge. The situation is described on sixty cards; they have to choose the number of cards they need to describe the measure they recommend. Each student works individually, and then we share the results and information required to determine the measure that will be recommended. There is no right or wrong answer.
   The students are confronted with the range of suggestions and the process for decision making. This exercise also increases self-awareness and the impact of our own values; we also suggest different ways to partly reduce subjectivity in decision making. The students also develop knowledge of the information needed to write a pre-disposition report.
2. Intervention Plan
   Using a pre-disposition report and the decision of the Court, the group works together to target the problem for intervention. Then one or two general and specific objectives are identified and discussed.
3. Exercises on presence and boundaries.
   This derives from the work of Jack Lee Rosenberg, Marjorie Rand and Diane Asay (1986) from the Institute of Integrative Body Psychotherapy.

The aim is to make students aware of their own and others' reactions to physical and emotional relationships. It begins with an exercise of concentration on how the student feels here and now. After that, breathing exercises are done to increase self-awareness and concentration. A group discussion follows this exercise.

Similarly, we suggest another integrative body exercise with distances and proximity. We want the students to experience how they react to closeness and distance and to be aware of their different reactions to their encounters with abandonment and/or invasion. We ask them to pair up. We suggest that student A draw a line around herself showing student B where she thinks their boundaries are. Then we ask student B to invade student A's boundaries. We have students pay close attention to their reactions, what they feel, how they feel and where the feelings are coming from. Student B is then asked to further invade student A's boundaries. Finally, we ask student A to return to her own boundaries. We suggest student A monitor how she regains physical space boundaries, personal reactions, feelings and physical attitudes. In a second part, we repeat the exercise, reversing roles of student A and B. At the end, we discuss each student's experiences in the exercise. We also ask students to give examples of situations where they experienced physical invasion of their boundaries with their clients or where they observed clients' resistance in response to closeness or distances in a meeting. We believe it is more instructive to experience this learning rather than to acquire it theoretically through reading or discussion. These exercises aim to develop student/worker self-awareness and control and to increase understanding of the clients' reactions or resistances to the process of intervention, which is a form of intrusion into their lives.

Four to six weeks after the beginning of the placements, we ask each student to produce an actual interview with a client on videotape and present this to the group. It is not an evaluation by the group. We watch it in sequences and use it as laboratory material. We do not permit negative criticism and ask for ideas on other ways to cope with similar situations. This also provides an occasion to discuss theories and techniques and to share work experiences on special issues (for example, sexual abuse) or other emotional situations that affect students.

The week before the end of the placement the students and field instructors meet to evaluate the experience they have had in the program. It is a chance for field instructors to receive feedback about the activities in the program, as well as for students to express and share feelings and thoughts about the field experimentation. Traditionally, students give their feedback about the changes they notice in their professional abilities and personal development. The field instructors observe a high level of satisfaction from students.

The goal of this paper was to describe a group supervision program. Although the service and setting are very precise, the program aims to teach the basic components of social work practice, the five steps of the intervention process and the helping relationship. In our program, experimentation and sharing of experiences are the two most important ways of learning. We believe this complements what the university offers to social work students in the classroom. The integration of knowledge, skills and self-awareness is our main objective. Even in a time of restraint, it remains essential in social work education to keep the focus on these elements.

References

Rosenberg, J.L.; Rand, M.L. & Asay, D. (1986). *Body, self and soul: Sustaining integration*. Atlanta (Georgia): Humanics Limited.

Rosenberg, J.L.; Rand, M.L. & Asay, D. (1989). *Le corps, le soi et l'âme*. Montréal: Québec Amérique.

Simon, P. & Albert, L. (1975). *Les relations interpersonnelles: Une approche expérientielle en milieu laboratoire*. Montréal: Agence d'ARC Inc.

Trépanier, J. (1984). "Le jeu de la décision" dans: *Les cahiers de l'école de criminologie*, cahier n°☐7. Université de Montréal.

Chapter 7

Starting Out:
Field Education in the Hinterland

Glen Schmidt

In 1994, the University of Northern British Columbia (UNBC) became the first new university to be established in Canada in over a quarter century. The development of social work field education within the context of a northern university presented a number of challenges. Factors that had to be considered included geography and economics, public attitudes toward social workers, and the unique nature of northern social work practice. The model that developed at UNBC may have some utility for social work programs that deliver field education to students in remote and isolated settings.

Geography and Economics

Northern British Columbia comprises an area of 632,762 square kilometres. Although larger than the European state of Germany, this part of B.C. has a comparatively small population of 314,380 people, representing about ten percent of the provincial total (Census Canada, 1991). Population density is sparse at one person per 2.01 square kilometres and population centres are generally separated by vast distances. Prince

George is the largest community with 81,000 people, and it is the home of UNBC's main campus. Officially, First Nations people account for eight percent of the region's population. However, the actual percentage is difficult to determine as a number of First Nations people and communities chose not to participate in the 1991 census. The real figure is probably closer to ten percent. Men outnumber women by about 4 percent and 12 percent of the population are new immigrants to Canada.

Throughout the region people depend upon resource-based industries for their livelihood. Mining, fishing, tourism and agriculture are key sectors, but the forestry industry stands out as the major employer. The central interior produces enough lumber to build 650,000 homes each year, a figure that is roughly three times the annual housing starts in all of Canada. (Guide to UNBC, 1995) Pulp mills, saw mills, and vast clear cut harvest areas are found throughout the northern British Columbia landscape.

The economic organization of the region produces effects not unlike those experienced by other northern parts of Canada, Scandinavia, Alaska, and Russia. Residents of the region are aware of the hinterland relationship with the lower mainland metropolis of Vancouver and the centralized and vertical organization of industry, government and services that result from this reality (Collier, 1993). Many northern resource-based communities across the country have a temporary quality about them, reinforced by the transient nature of the population and what the Davenports (1980) referred to as the visible bifurcation between newcomers and established residents.

This is the case with boom towns or impact communities that tend to attract a mobile, predominantly male, labour force. Lucas (1971) first described the process of resource-based community evolution in his classic work *Minetown Milltown Railtown*. In northern B.C. there is a long list of communities that have followed this pattern of development, and there are also a number of communities that have disappeared or experienced significant decline as the boom has ended or demand for the sustaining resource has disappeared. The asbestos mining town of Cassiar is one of the most recent casualties, a company town that was completely shut down in 1992.

A pioneering type of culture tends to emerge from the geographic and economic influences, and education has not always been a priority in a region where people can earn a good income working in resource industries. In 1989, when a university planning and implementation group first began to advise the Minister of Advanced Education, Training and Technology, the minister of the day was quoted in the *Globe and Mail*: "In the interior (of B.C.) people don't think of education beyond Grade 12. The questions they ask at the end of the day are: How many trees did you cut today? or How were things down in the mine?" (October 2, 1989). This minister's attitude did not necessarily represent the views of all northern people, and in 1994, the University of Northern British Columbia was officially opened with broad public support. Social work was among the 23 undergraduate programs offered by the new university.

The Provincial Context for the Social Work Profession

The establishment of the social work program at UNBC occurred at a time when the profession received unprecedented media coverage in British Columbia. This was a direct result of the *Report of the Gove Inquiry into Child Protection* (1995) and the hearings leading up to the release of the *Gove Report*. Unfortunately the publicity surrounding this review was negative and the public image of social work took a considerable battering (Callahan, 1997).

The Gove Inquiry involved a wide ranging examination of child welfare practice prompted by the 1992 death of five-year-old Matthew Vaudreuil, who was murdered by his mother. The tragic death and subsequent investigation led to a critical examination of child welfare practice in the Province of British Columbia. Questionable internal reviews and allegations of a cover up resulted in calls for an external investigation into the circumstances leading to the death of young Matthew. Judge Thomas Gove was appointed to head the resulting inquiry. The findings of his report raised serious concerns about child welfare social work practice. According to the documentation provided to the Gove Inquiry, Matthew Vaudreuil had contact with 21 social workers and 24 physicians during his brief life. His mother, who had herself been a child in care, sometimes sought assistance and support in parenting Matthew, who presented with difficult tantrums, malnutrition and self-abusive behaviour.

The end result of all this was public vilification of the social work profession. Questions regarding educational standards, competence, regulation and values were raised by the media as well as the public. A challenge for social work at UNBC related to the fact that Matthew and his mother originally lived in Fort St. John, a major community in the northeastern part of UNBC's territory.

Northern Social Work

The needs of northern social work education differ substantially from education for urban-based practice. In northern and remote social work, specialization in practice and access to specialized services are limited and social work education must have a stronger focus on the generalist model. The nature of the practice itself requires students to understand the Code of Ethics and professional conduct in ways that do not necessarily meet an urban standard (Brownlee, 1996; Delaney, Brownlee, Sellick & Tranter, 1997). This is particularly the case around issues such as dual relationships and confidentiality. Dual relationships are inevitable in a small isolated town or reserve and the worker's ability to adjust to the strains involved under these circumstances will have a direct impact on their capacity and willingness to stay in the community (Schmidt, 1994). Work in small communities and work in First Nations communities using child welfare committees, elders and healing circles also pushes the limit of expectations around confidentiality.

Research conducted for the Gove Inquiry revealed that the academic qualifications of social workers employed by the Ministry of Social Services vary from north to south. Provincially, 46 percent of MSS social workers did not have any social work training. In the northern region, this figure rose to 54 percent, a difference of 8 percent from the provincial figure. Information is not available for the large, non-government contract sector, but wages are often lower, and people with social work degrees are less likely to enter this type of employment. Higher rates of social worker turnover and historic difficulty in gaining access to BSW programs are likely reasons for the lower number of BSW social workers in the northern part of the province. This situation is not unique to British Columbia as other provinces and the Canadian territories often experience difficulty in the recruitment and retention of professionally qualified social workers.

Challenges and Barriers for Field Education

In the development of a new program there are clearly some advantages as well as disadvantages. It is advantageous to be able to cast about for what has worked in similar situations and also identify and avoid what has been problematic. Material was gathered from across the country and manuals, assignments, evaluations and other useful field information were reviewed before developing the UNBC program.

Field education provides a critical link between academic social work and the practice community (Bogo & Globerman, 1995; Black, 1996; Bogo & Vayda, 1998). If trust and credibility are created through this linkage, then the practice community is likely to have confidence in the more purely academic components of the program. Alternative views and new ideas gain credibility when students demonstrate an effective approach to beginning practice. If the goals of field education are not understood and students lack rudimentary skills, competencies, and knowledge to begin social work, the practice community will quickly become critical of the academic social work program. Field education coordinators and their students are an important component in the relationship between academic social work and the practice community. They form the bridge and the link.

With this in mind, the first step in the development of field education was to meet with as many members of the practice community and agencies as possible. Meetings revolved around general information sharing regarding the program and the inevitable question about whether they would be willing to take a field student. Some of the practitioners and organizations had experience with field education students through other institutions. It was important to hear what had been positive about these experiences and what might be improved. People and agencies who had provided supervision consistently expressed a need for more contact with the educational institution and greater clarity around expectations. Despite these concerns it was clear that practitioners and agencies enjoyed having students in their midst. During recruitment interviews, agency workers reported that students often brought new ideas and enthusiasm to the workplace which, in turn, revitalized experienced practitioners.

During the meetings it also became apparent that meeting requirement 3.3.1 Appendix F of the Canadian Association of Schools of Social Work Accreditation Standards was going to be difficult. This requirement states that:

> Field instructors at the BSW level should possess, at a minimum, a BSW degree from a recognized professional program and two years of social work practice experience after graduation.

Many agencies did not employ BSW social workers and this was often the case in agencies delivering service to First Nations people. Given the emphasis in accreditation standards on delivering social work education that is anti-racist and meets the service needs of ethnically diverse groups, it became important to ensure that the agencies devoted to serving diverse populations were not eliminated from the field education process. Fortunately Section 3.3.3 of Appendix F states that:

> Under certain circumstances, BSW and MSW degree level field instruction may be carried out by persons who have not achieved a professional social work degree. In such circumstances, it is expected that the school will play a greater role in the monitoring and supervision of the field experience to assure that a social work focus is sustained and that the student has access to a qualified social worker. Alternatively, a faculty member may be designated as the field instructor.

Given the resource constraints experienced by social work at UNBC, it was impossible to move to a faculty field instruction model. However, the accreditation standard clearly indicates that it is essential to have the social work program play a greater role in supervision of the field experience when workers lacking appropriate education and experience are providing supervision.

While there were many agency supervisors who had some experience with students there were also many more who had no experience with student supervision and the teaching aspect that is so vital. This also became a consideration in setting up the program and ensuring the BSW at UNBC would meet accreditation expectations under Section 3.4 - Preparation of Field Instructors.

A final consideration in the early exploratory work revolved around the number of students, number of agencies and the projected longer-term impact of constantly going back to agencies for placements. The smaller population and number of communities found in northern locations also meant that there were fewer agencies in which to place students.

The Field Education Program at UNBC

The information that emerged from the early exploratory work was important and helped to identify issues and goals that would be critical in setting up the field education program. A major issue was that an agency-based field instruction model would not work. There simply were not enough qualified BSW instructors available. At the same time the amount of program funding from the university would not allow for faculty-based field instruction. This is an expensive and labour intensive model which has been largely abandoned by social work programs.

One goal that resulted from meetings with agencies was recognition of the importance of presenting a well-organized program with clear lines of communication. Both organization and clear communication tend to emerge over time, but in the case of UNBC, it was very important to quickly address these matters to establish credibility.

Another issue was that agency supervisors would require support and information as well as validation to keep them engaged in the process of field education. Above all, their contribution could not be taken for granted.

Given these considerations, the model of instruction chosen by UNBC was a hybrid type of model which blended faculty and agency-based instruction. This was necessary for two reasons: the need to address accreditation standards and the need to provide close support and consistent communication for the agency-based instructors.

1995-1996: Year 1 of the UNBC Field Education Program

The first cohort of students, numbering 24, was divided into two field sections, and they met every two weeks for a half-day integrative seminar. The seminars provided information on selected topics, opportunity for skill practice, and a time to discuss professional and ethical issues that developed during the course of the student placements.

Evaluation of assignments was taken on by the faculty advisor to ease the workload for the agency supervisors. However, agency supervisors were welcome to be a part of this process with the student's consent.

The actual evaluation of students was a collaborative process involving three parties. The student produced a self-evaluation based upon a critical analysis of performance and achievement of learning contract goals; the student and agency supervisor developed a competency-based evaluation, again based upon the learning contract and agency expectations; and the faculty advisor produced an evaluation based upon the student assignments and the student integration of practice and theory. All three partners met and a written summary narrative was produced by the faculty advisor and shared with the other two partners.

At a minimum, the agency supervisor, student and faculty advisor had three face-to-face meetings. The first meeting was to approve the learning goals and the second and third meetings dealt with the mid-term and final evaluations. Although three formal face-to-face contacts were the minimum number during the 13 week term, over 50 percent of the placements had more than three meetings. This was necessary to solve problems in placements or to complete a more extensive evaluation process.

Assessing the First Year

A number of points bear consideration in assessing outcomes after the first year of operation. The first was the rate of attrition between the time of initial agency recruitment and actual confirmation of placement. Forty placements were recruited during the spring and summer of 1995, but when it was time to confirm the placement in September, a total of ten (or 25 percent) of the placements were no longer available. The primary reason given for the attrition was an increase in work load that made it impossible for the supervisor to take a student.

Of the 40 placements that were recruited, five were situated out of town. Among these, four involved a one-hour commute to towns located relatively close to Prince George. However, the only out-of-town placement that was selected by a student was located two hours to the west. The critical factor for this student seemed to be finances. The student who selected the out-of-town placement reported doing this because staying with family in the community made it affordable. For other students, placements outside the main educational centre were difficult. The BSW student population is made up of many people who are mature students and have children at home. Longer days and trips out of town obviously present problems. The university's inability to subsidize placements also created financial challenges for students, most of whom are on a limited income. As a result, regional placements are not attractive to students.

A further surprise was the fact that there were no major disasters in this first year of operation. With a new university, agency supervisors and program, there was an expectation of difficulty. While some placements were disappointing and did not offer students the best quality of field education, the majority were ranked positively and the placement proceeded without incident. Roles were clearly defined in orientation and training and this potential area of difficulty did not result in any problems.

Evaluation

Evaluation outcomes from students and instructors were almost all positive, judging by returned questionnaires. The evaluation questions focused on several critical areas. It was important to get a sense of the students' experiences of the placement. Second, it was very important to understand the agency supervisors' experience of student supervision and the UNBC social work program. The evaluation forms that were used allowed for narrative and explanatory commentary but also left room for simple "yes" and "no" answers in most instances.

Eighteen of the 24 students completed the field evaluation questionnaires for a response rate of 75 percent. The questionnaire was strictly voluntary, as is the case with all instructor/course evaluations at UNBC. Fifteen of the respondents were female and three were male. Ten questions were used to evaluate the students' experience of field education with the UNBC social work program. These questions related to the university as well as the agency. Particular attention was devoted to determining whether students' learning needs were met and if they felt comfortable within the agency setting. The responses are displayed in Table 1.

Thirteen of the agency supervisor/instructors completed the field education evaluation forms. As three of the students had two supervisors this represented a response rate under 50 percent (13 of 27). Agency supervisors responded to eight questions that focused on their experience of supervising a student; they were also asked to evaluate the role of the university, as well as material resources and training provided by the university. The results are summarized in Table 2.

Table 1
Student Field Education Evaluation

Question	Yes	No	Partial/NR
1. Did the actual learning opportunity fit the preliminary description of this placement?	13 (72.2%)	3 (16.7%)	2 partial
2. As a student, did you feel accepted in the agency or organization?	18 (100%)	0	0
3. Was the agency field instructor accessible and approachable?	17 (94.4%)	1 (5.6%)	0
4. Did the agency field instructor demonstrate an understanding of your learning needs and goals in terms of the UNBC social work program?	17 (94.4%)	1 (5.6%)	0
5. Were the work expectations clear and unambiguous for you?	15 (83.3%)	0	3 partial
6. Was contact with the faculty instructor adequate?	15 (83.3%)	1 (5.6%)	2 no response
7. Did the faculty instructor demonstrate knowledge of the practice issues you faced in this agency?	16 (88.9%)	1 (5.6%)	1 no response
8. Overall, how would you rate this placement?	10 excellent 1 very good 1 satisfactory 1 poor 5 nr		
9. Would you recommend it for other students?	17 (94.4%)	1 (5.6%)	0
10. What changes should be made?	4 space (22.2%)		

Table 2
Agency Field Instructor Evaluation of Field Education

Question	Yes	No
1. Was communication with the UNBC social work program adequate?	13 (100%)	0
2. Was the purpose of the placement clear to you?	13 (100%)	0
3. Did you receive adequate and appropriate information from the university?	13 (100%)	0
4. Did having a student create any time management or workload management difficulties for you?	6 (46%)	7 (54%)
5. Was contact with the faculty instructor adequate and useful?	13 (100%)	0
6. Overall, how would you rate your experience of supervising a social work student?	All said good or superior. One respondent noted this was more positive than any other supervision experience.	
7. Would you consider taking a student again?	13 (100%)	0
8. What changes would you recommend?	Most changes related to agencies. No response pattern emerged. The one recommended change for UNBC has to do with clearer labelling of evaluation forms.	

Discussion

The comments of respondents are generally positive. The data suggest some need to clarify the preliminary information material distributed to students. It was also clear that a number of students see space as an issue. However, this is not within the control of the university, nor is it something that agencies can easily change.

Significantly, all but one of the placements were given a positive recommendation. It was also important to see that agency supervisors and faculty advisors were generally given a good rating. The low response rate from agency supervisors is a limitation, but regular contact with the supervisors suggests that satisfaction with the program was widespread even among those who did not return a questionnaire.

Summary: What was learned?

Some important lessons can be derived from the development of this field education program. First, it was important to develop regular and consistent communication with agency supervisors. This is critical when many of the supervisors do not have social work degrees, as is the case in northern British Columbia. Regular communication helps to identify problems, and it enables the faculty liaison person to provide social work input into placements where someone other than a social worker is providing the supervision.

Second, enthusiasm on the part of agencies for field education placements does not translate into actual spots. Staff turnover, funding changes, and internal reorganization are regular events that consistently alter the best plans. Turnover in northern agencies is particularly high, and this contributed to the 25 percent loss in recruited placements.

Third, the realities of social work in the hinterland created the necessity for faculty involvement in the instruction of field students. Program resources did not allow for a pure faculty-based model of instruction, nor is this seen as the optimum alternative. The UNBC hybrid model allows for substantial agency contribution, while addressing the needs around accreditation. Even with the "hybrid" model it is important for the university to provide adequate resources for the delivery of field education.

Finally, clear goals, consistent organization and a collaborative approach yield positive results in terms of outcome evaluations. In perilous times, agencies and agency personnel require predictability and clarity regarding the university's expectations. The primary responsibility for achieving this result rests with the field education coordinator and the faculty involved in field liaison.

References

Black. J. (1996). Between the agency and the university. *Reflections, 2*(3): 31-33.

Bogo, M. & Globerman, J. (1995). Creating effective university-field partnerships: An analysis of two inter-organization models for field education. *Journal of Teaching in Social Work, 11*(1/2). 177-92.

Bogo, M., & Vayda, E. (1998). *The practice of field instruction in social work* (2nd ed.). Toronto: University of Toronto Press.

Brownlee, K. (1996). Ethics in community care: The ethics of non-sexual dual relationships: A dilemma for the rural mental health professional. *Community Mental Health Journal, 32*(5), 497-503.

Callahan, M., & Callahan, K. (1997). Victims and villains: Scandals, the press and policy making in child welfare. In J. Pulkingham & G. Ternowetsky (Eds.), *Child and family policies: Struggles, strategies and options* (pp. 40-57). Halifax: Fernwood Publishing.

Canadian Association of Schools of Social Work. (1993). Board of accreditation manual of educational policy statements accreditation standards and procedures for schools of social work (Revised Edition). Author.

Collier, K. (1993). *Social work with rural peoples* (2nd ed.). Vancouver: New Star Books.

Davenport, J. & Davenport, J. (1980). Grits and other preventive measures for boomtown bifurcation. In J. Davenport & J. Davenport (Eds.) *The boom town: Problems and promises in the energy vortex* (pp. 43-53). Laramie: University of Wyoming Department of Social Work.

Delaney, R., Brownlee, K., Sellick, M., & Tranter, D. (1997). Ethical problems facing northern social workers. *The Social Worker, 65*(3), 55-65.

Gove, T. (1995). *Report of the Gove inquiry into child protection in British Columbia*. Vancouver, B.C.: Government Publications.

Government of Canada (1992). *Census Canada, 1991*. Ottawa: Statistics Canada.

UNBC. *Guide to UNBC*. (May, 1995).

Lucas, R. (1971). *Minetown milltown railtown*. Toronto: University of Toronto Press.

Schmidt, G. (1994, February). *Issues, challenges and dilemmas facing social workers in northern and remote practice*. Paper presented at a public meeting for UNBC and the BCASW.

UNBC. *UNBC Planning Committee: Preliminary Report*. (May 1, 1996).

SECTION III

LINKAGES & EXCHANGES BETWEEN FIELD SETTINGS AND THE UNIVERSITY

Chapter 8

Strengthening the Integration of Research, Teaching, and Practice in Graduate Programs: An Academic Field-Partnership Model

Judith Globerman
Marion Bogo

P rofessional programs in universities have experienced changing expectations from the university with regards to the importance of scholarship and research. Schools of social work have been challenged to enhance their faculty members' contributions to scholarship. Defining the school's research mission in relation to social work and social welfare has been a priority. Research is expected to contribute to knowledge for practice, programs, and policy and to strengthen the nexus between research, teaching, and practice. Therefore, the research of faculty members must be grounded and take place in the "real world" of the community. To achieve this mission, teaching faculty are needed who can integrate teaching, research, and practice and can bridge the university and the community. A partnership model for linking the university and the community is presented that meets the university's research and teaching mission, advances student learning opportunities, and enhances collaboration and communication between the university and the community.

Mission of Graduate Schools

With a greater emphasis on scholarship and research, faculty in graduate programs have experienced increased expectations for productivity in these areas, especially in the past decade (Gibbs & Locke, 1989; Wheeler & Gibbons, 1992). A focus on the knowledge- building enterprise in social work and social welfare has led schools to hire faculty with doctorate degrees and research expertise (Feld, 1988). Similar to other academic disciplines, the expectation is that these academics will contribute to scholarship through research and publication. The aim is "... to engage in more research that addresses critical practice and policy questions in the field, builds collaborative partnerships with community agencies and simultaneously enriches the teaching and service missions of schools" (McMahon, Reisch, & Patti, 1991, p. 18). To realize this, social work educators need to pay more attention to the integration of research, teaching, and practice. Since social work education is in the unique position of taking place in two environments — the university and the community — a natural vehicle already exists for this integration.

Faculty-Field Liaison Model

Social work programs traditionally have established structures to connect the two aspects of the educational program to ensure effective preparation for professional practice. The primary mechanism to provide this link has been the faculty-field liaison. Although there is not one universal liaison model there are common core functions and roles for faculty-field liaison in schools of social work (Brownstein, Smith, & Faria, 1991; Fortune, Miller, Rosenblum, Sanchez, Smith, & Reid, 1995; Raphael & Rosenblum, 1987; Raskin, 1994; Smith, Faria, & Brownstein, 1986). According to Smith and colleagues' (1986) empirical study of 54 American accredited MSW programs, the core functions and roles that exist in all sampled schools include linkage, monitoring, consulting, mediating, evaluating, and holding of administrative responsibilities. Although maintaining university-field partnerships has been a key objective, the findings that roles of faculty field liaison are primarily centred on monitoring, mediating and evaluating students and field instructors emphasizes the differences between theory and practice (Raskin, 1994). Practice focuses much more on student-instructor relationships and student learning than on inter-organization relations and linkage between the university and field agencies. Structures to enhance inter-organization relationships have received little attention in the literature (Bogo & Globerman, 1995; Frumkin, 1980).

The primary focus on field education as the bridge between the university and the field agencies has proven to be problematic. In graduate programs, field education is generally managed by a "practicum director" or co-ordinator who is responsible for the administrative and workload requirements of the program and the assigning of individuals to field liaison roles (Hawthorne & Holtzman, 1991; Smith et al., 1986). The focus of these assignments has consistently been to bridge the gap between the agencies who offer student practica and the university. In practice, practicum education has been relegated, at times, to "second-class citizen" in graduate programs where the emphasis is on knowledge development through research (Gantt, Pinsky, Rock, & Rosenberg, 1990; Grossman, 1991; Hartman, 1990; Raskin, 1994). Practicum directors, field education co-ordinators, and faculty-field liaisons are frequently non-tenure stream instructors and professors without PhD degrees who are in teaching and practice streams in programs whereas other professors teaching academic courses have PhD degrees and tenure and manage research careers (Brownstein et al., 1991; Hawthorne & Holtzman, 1991; Jones, 1984).

The identification of practicum education as requiring a different model — a non-academic model — as evidenced by the requirements of lesser qualifications, is paradoxical. The integration of research, teaching, and practice is touted as the essence of graduate social work education (Gantt et al., 1990; Kilpatrick, 1991; Wheeler & Gibbons, 1992). An effective bridge between the academy and the agency is considered critical to realizing this integration. Yet those with the knowledge to set in motion and control this integration, the practicum co-ordinators, are not the power brokers in the school; they are the least powerful and least valued, according to the standards of the academy which place funded research and publications at the pinnacle (Brownstein et al., 1991; Hawthorne & Holtzman, 1991). Furthermore, in the traditional model the practicum co-ordinators' focus has been on students' learning in the field rather than the integration of research, teaching, and practice.

The field education experts who participated in Raskin's (1994) Delphi study of field education achieved strong consensus on the statement that "field education is not considered academic" (p. 82). They call for new models of faculty-field liaison that address the needs for the integration of research, teaching, and practice. As stated by one research participant: "Is it not time to start discussing and developing new models that meet educational goals and that faculty feel committed to enacting?" (p. 87)

Research in Practice Settings

Increasingly, social work leaders and practice researchers are convinced that the knowledge-building enterprise of the profession requires grounded research, expanded and tested practice models, and rigorous explorations of social issues (Caputo, 1985; Epstein & Grellong, 1992; Hess & Mullen, 1995; McMahon et al., 1991). Obviously this research must take place in practice settings and involve the two sites, the setting and the university, in a close partnership to ensure relevance and feasibility of the research. The agency will benefit from new knowledge to improve service delivery, while the academic will be informed by the demands of social issues and needs in the construction of a knowledge base for theory, practice and policy. Greater research dissemination and utilization is likely to occur when practitioners are part of knowledge discovery and findings are easily accessible and can be used to address daily practice challenges. Academics engaged in grounded research in field agencies are likely to integrate emerging findings in their current teaching. Insofar as there are links between the practicum and academic courses, the integration of research, teaching, and practice for students will be strengthened.

Fraser (1994), in a review of the challenges facing social work research, draws attention to the findings of numerous studies that social workers rarely use the literature when confronted with a practice problem. He strongly recommends that researchers give attention to the complicated tasks of transmitting applied knowledge and suggests reconceptualizing faculty "service" as "... the systematic and scholarly application of the profession's knowledge base to a community problem" (p. 263). Schneck (1991a) challenges field education to take leadership: "... field education could become the primary medium for the bridge between the university function to generate knowledge and innovation (the educational ideal) and the professional function to apply and refine knowledge in specific practice applications (the practice reality)" (p. 29).

This vision of strong links between the university and the service organization for research relies, for its success, on processes and activities that build effective inter-organization relations. These are the result of effective communication, reciprocity, respect, and collaborative activities

(Bogo & Globerman, 1995; Schneck, 1991b). In summary, as the expectations of teaching faculty in graduate social work programs has changed, an efficient model to link the university and the practice community has not yet emerged. What is required is a model that unites the university's research and teaching mission; the research interests of individual teaching faculty; students' needs for vehicles to help them integrate research, theory, and practice; and the field's needs for new knowledge and evaluation to document effectiveness to funders. A new conceptualization of the role and function of a faculty member to provide linkage is, therefore, a necessity.

An Academic-Field Partnership Model

A new model to bridge the university and the community agencies is described that addresses the current knowledge-building expectations in universities, the sophisticated knowledge and skill of field educators, and the growing interest in and recognition of the need for integration of research, practice, and teaching. The goal is true partnership between the academic educators and the field educators. The model rests on principles for effective inter-organization relations and aims to develop inter-organization relations that (a) enhance the field education program, (b) develop collaborative and reciprocal opportunities for research and teaching, and (c) develop and maintain communication between the university and the organization.

This new conceptualization of university linkage incorporates models of faculty-field liaison currently in existence (Fortune et al., 1995; Raphael & Rosenblum, 1987; Smith et al., 1986). Rosenblum & Raphael (1983, p. 69) described the liaison role as involving "building, maintaining, and traversing an imaginary bridge" between the school of social work and the agency. An academic-field partnership model expands this image by adding a new lane to the bridge to reflect the complex activities that need to go beyond student education to support the knowledge-building enterprise of the profession. The bridge now consists of two major functions. The first involves field education and emphasizes activities to enhance student-field instructor relations, the primary factor contributing to a positive field experience. Consistent with Fortune and Abramson's (1993) recommendation that liaisons are more effective as consultants to field instructors than as monitors of students or field instructors, and with Fortune and colleagues' (1995) finding that field instructors consider teaching-related activities of the liaison to be the most important, this function de-emphasizes the monitoring, overseer role and enhances the role of consultant, facilitator and troubleshooter. The second function is a new component which relates to furthering the integration of research, teaching and practice through effective inter-organization relations.

The proposed partnership model of faculty-university linkage for graduate social work programs emphasizes this second function. It involves faculty, those who hold tenure and funded research, with field agencies. It integrates the field education component of Masters programs into all faculty members' workloads, placing co-ordination responsibility into the hands of a faculty member with seniority or currency in the university. Lodging direction of the practicum with a tenured faculty position places the practicum on an even footing with the other academic administrative leaders such as the Director of the Doctoral Program. As such, the faculty member responsible for the practicum component of the students' education is a member of the school's administrative management group and has the power and influence to assign faculty to liaison responsibilities and to further the relationship between the field component and the course curriculum. In this academic model, faculty are responsible to this Director or Academic Co-ordinator of the Practicum for performance in this role.

Enhanced Field Education Program

The aim of the new model is to enhance social work education through the integration of teaching, research, and practice. While classroom courses attempt to achieve this goal, the field education component is often marginalized and separated from the academic discourse (Vayda & Bogo, 1991). However, the field education program is the logical location for the integration of research, teaching, and practice, since it is the site for grounding research and testing the efficacy of models and theories in action. Appreciating that students experience their field practice education as primary, the enhancement of this component through greater involvement of all faculty is critical. Findings from empirical research conclude that students perceive the relationship with the field instructor as the critical factor in promoting student learning and satisfaction in the practicum (Fortune & Abramson, 1993; Fortune, Feathers, Rook, Scrimenti, Smollen, Stemerman, & Tucker, 1985; Tolson & Kopp, 1988) and that having tasks and assignments that were meaningful to the student and grounded in both the agency and inter-organization relations influenced students' satisfaction with practica (Neugeboren, 1988). Necessary elements that contribute to the relationship are emotional support, autonomy-giving behaviour which encourages independence and the student's active participation in learning, ongoing specific and constructive feedback about the student's performance, and cognitive structuring which helps the student link theory and practice and provides information and explanations that help clarify practice issues and interventions (Bogo, 1993; Fortune & Abramson, 1993). These findings have implications for school policies and practices for developing field educators.

When schools of social work recruit new field instructors they seek out competent social workers with an interest in contributing to the profession through educating students. Schools recognize and respect the expertise of these social work practitioners and offer training to provide them with the necessary knowledge, skill, and support to function as effective social work educators in the field. Based on the empirical findings discussed above, it is particularly important that the new field instructors are aware of the importance of their behaviours and the impact they have on promoting student learning. Given the centrality of the student and field instructor relationship, a primary task of the faculty in the new partnership model is to support and facilitate the field instructor through consultation and trouble shooting. This shifts the faculty role from the traditional liaison role of monitoring and supervising to a collegial partnership between two educators, one in the university and one in the practice setting. This notion is similar to that proposed by Fortune and Abramson (1993) that faculty field liaisons function more as consultants to field instructors and place less emphasis on monitoring students.

In the new partnership model presented here the primary function of the faculty member emanates from their expertise in knowledge building. The faculty member can help the field instructor integrate practice with theory and research. Although graduate programs usually have courses in social work theory and practice, the research suggests that integration of theory and practice occurs in the field (Tolson & Kopp, 1988). Thus, the field educators have considerable responsibility for this integration, and the faculty have the primary responsibility for linking the field with the classroom and research knowledge. The mechanism to achieve this integration is to assign graduate faculty to field agencies. For example, faculty engaged in practice research in mental health at the micro level would be assigned to clinical mental health agencies; those engaged in community-based action research would be assigned to community centres and grass roots organizations; faculty engaged in policy research would be assigned to governmental, non-governmental, and planning organizations. Matching faculty to agencies directly connected to their field of research is the first step towards bridging practice learning, classroom experiences, and research.

In summary, while part of the faculty responsibility still involves consulting with the field instructor to facilitate field learning, in this model, with faculty integrally connected to agencies linked to their scholarship, their role is expanded. They now play a key role in integrating practice with research and teaching. The result is more relevant teaching, more grounded research, and students integrating research with practice with greater facility and skill.

Collaborative Opportunities
for Teaching and Research

Professors in graduate social work programs are expected to have programs of research. These research agendas involve the academic community in social work and social welfare research linked to both governmental and non-governmental policy, community and clinical settings. The linkage between faculty research and faculty field liaison activities has not been formally addressed in schools of social work. As a result, two levels of inter-organization relations exist: those between the faculty and their research sites or contacts, and those between liaisons and field settings.

In the current academic environment, with shrinking resources, larger enrolments, fewer academic staff, and fewer teaching assistants, increasing faculty responsibilities in linkages with the field settings for field education is unlikely to be seen as a priority by faculty in graduate programs. However, faculty are already integrally connected to field settings by virtue of their practice and research responsibilities. Thus, it is to the faculty that we turn for the development of inter-organization relations. These relations have multiple purposes. Not only do they provide opportunities to develop collaborative and reciprocal relations for research and teaching, but they enhance the field education program, and the development and maintenance of communication between the university and the community.

The result is a more complex relationship than that built solely on the faculty member's research relationship. In this integrated academic partnership model, faculty are assigned responsibilities with agencies with whom they are encouraged to establish long-term collaborative relations based on both the faculty member's research agenda and the organization's service mandate. This gives the faculty member institutional sanction for participation with the field. It also provides an opportunity to develop relationships that will lead to grounded practice research, to understand the context for students' experiences and classroom practice examples, and to learn about practice from the field educators and practitioners. The linkage role thus expands from that of mediator and consultant to that of collaborator and partner.

In keeping with the partnership model that emphasizes and respects the researcher and academic as well as the field educator's expertise, faculty members do not monitor field instruction. Their responsibility is to be the link between the educational program and the student's field practicum. As such they work in collaboration with the field educator to link theory with practice, keeping the field educator abreast of changes in the research literature and concurrently researching changing practice.

Communication Between the University and the Organization

Typically when there are difficulties in the field, the faculty field liaison is used as a mediator between the university and the field setting for the student and the field instructor, and as a partner to help problem solve. The effectiveness of a faculty field liaison at problem-solving or trouble-shooting has much to do with the nature of the inter-organization relationships, particularly the trust and respect between the two organizations. This new model is built on the notion of equal partnership between the collaborating organizations in social work education, the university and the field agency. Each has expertise the other needs and wants, and each can contribute to the richness of the other. As discussed above, this exists more in theory than in practice. The proposed model places collaborative relationships at the forefront and emphasizes the need for inter-organization communication.

An enhanced partnership model has the advantage of improving communication and collaboration through linking agencies with each other through the university. As graduate faculty are assigned to field agencies linked to their research interests, they have the opportunity to link students and agencies together. Depending on their practice and research objectives and the school's priorities, these linkages could be for integrative seminars, research projects, or to address common issues. Several examples at the Faculty of Social Work, University of Toronto demonstrate the enhanced communication this model encourages. In one situation, health settings and faculty members in the health field meet as a research consortium to study health care practice issues in social work (Bogo et al., 1992). As program management in the health field became a critical issue for social workers, these inter-organization relations provided the opportunity for a faculty member to research hospital restructuring. In another example, a faculty member with research interests in child welfare was assigned several child protection agencies. He elected to bring the practicum students together for informal uncredited integrative seminars so they could receive mutual support and augment their learning about other settings. This allowed the faculty member to become more familiar with their field instructors, the agencies' policies, programs, and current issues, which, in turn, enhanced the inter-organization communication. In another example, to facilitate a graduate collaborative program in women's studies, the social work faculty representative on the collaborative program committee was assigned six feminist agencies; although this faculty member had little social work faculty field liaison experience, she had extensive feminist research expertise and good connections to the feminist social work community, As a result of this assignment and her direct involvement in learning about the students' field education, she has become a communication link between these agencies and the school and a major contributor to developing feminist field practica for the Masters program.

This academic partnership model is successful because of its respect for the complexity of inter-organization relations. To maintain effective practica, the university must become partners with the field settings. Social work practice is complex and demanding, and students' experiences in the field must be managed by faculty and practicum staff who are involved in the teaching of theory, practice and research courses. Faculty who are actively engaged in research and teaching must be integrally involved with the field program.

Conclusion

The challenge for social work educators in graduate programs is to unite the goal of integration of research, teaching and practice with our knowledge of the process and value of field education and inter-organization relations. By strengthening and expanding linkage functions beyond a student focus to include the institutional priority of knowledg-building, both student education and the integration of research, teaching and practice can be enhanced. For decades the profession of social work has engaged in knowledge building to support responsible practice. The partnership model presented here enhances this endeavour through its championing of the expertise of educators both in the field and the university.

References

Bogo, M. (1993). The student/field instructor relationship: The critical factor in field education. *The Clinical Supervisor, 11*(2):23-36.

Bogo, M. & Globerman, J. (1995). Creating effective university-field partnerships: An analysis of two inter-organization models. *Journal of Teaching in Social Work, 11*(1/2):177-192.

Bogo, M.; Wells, L.; Abbey, S.; Bergman, A.; Chandler, V.; Embleton, L.; Guirgis, S.; Huot, A.; McNeill, T.; Prentice, L.; Stapleton, D.; Shekter-Wolfson; L. & Urman, S. (1992). Advancing social work practice in the health field: A collaborative research partnership. *Health & Social Work, 17*(3):223-235.

Brownstein, C.; Smith, H.Y. & Faria, G. (1991). The liaison role: A three phase study of the schools, the field, the faculty. In D. Schneck; B. Grossman & U. Glassman (Eds.) *Field education in social work: Contemporary issues and trends.* (237-248). Dubuque, Iowa: Kendall/Hunt.

Caputo, R. (1985). The role of research in the family service agency. *Social Casework, 66*(4):205-212.

Epstein, I. & Grellong, B.A. (1992). Models of university-agency collaboration in research. *Research on Social Work Practice, 2*(3):350-357.

Feld, S. (1988). The academic marketplace in social work. *Journal of Social Work Education, 24*(3):201-210.

Fortune, A.E. & Abramson, J.S. (1993). Predictors of satisfaction with field practicum among social work students. *The Clinical Supervisor, 11*(1):95-110.

Fortune, A.; Feathers, C.; Rook, S.; Scrimenti, R.; Smollen, P.; Stemerman, B. & Tucker, E. (1985). Student satisfaction with field placement. *Journal of Social Work Education, 21*(3):92-104.

Fortune, A.E.; Miller, J.; Rosenblum, A.F.; Sanchez, B.M.; Smith, C. & Reid, W.J. (1995). Further explorations of the liaison role: A view from the field. In G. Rogers (Ed.) *Social work field education: Views and visions* (273-293). Dubuque, Iowa: Kendall/Hunt.

Fraser, M. (1994). Scholarship and research in social work: Emerging challenges. *Journal of Social Work Education, 30*(2):252-266.

Frumkin, M. (1980). Social work education and the professional commitment fallacy: A practical guide to field-school relations. *Journal of Education for Social Work, 16*(2):91-99.

Gantt, A.; Pinsky, S.; Rock, B. & Rosenberg, E. (1990). Practice and research: An integrative approach. *Journal of Teaching in Social Work, 4*(1):129-143.

Gibbs, P. & Locke, B. (1989). Tenure and promotion in accredited graduate social work programs. *Journal of Social Work Education, 25*(2):126-133.

Grossman, B. (1991). Themes and variations: The political economy of field instruction. In D. Schneck, B. Grossman & U. Glassman (Eds.) *Field education in social work: Contemporary issues and trends.* (36-41). Dubuque, Iowa: Kendall/Hunt.

Hartman, A. (1990). Education for direct practice. *Families in Society: The Journal of Contemporary Human Services, 71*:44-50.

Hawthorne, L. & Holtzman, R.F. (1991). Directors of field education: Critical role dilemmas. In D. Schneck, B. Grossman & U. Glassman (Eds.) *Field education in social work: Contemporary issues and trends.* (320-328). Dubuque, Iowa: Kendall/Hunt.

Hess, P. M. & Mullen E. J. (1995). *Practitioner-researcher partnerships: Building knowledge from, in, and for practice.* Washington, D.C.: NASW Press.

Jones, E.F. (1984). Square peg, round hole: The dilemma of the undergraduate social work field co-ordinator. *Journal of Education for Social Work, 20*:45-50.

Kilpatrick, A.C. (1991). Differences and commonalities in BSW and MSW field instruction: In search of continuity. In D. Schneck, B. Grossman & U. Glassman (Eds.) *Field education in social work: Contemporary issues and trends.* (167-176). Dubuque, Iowa: Kendall/Hunt.

McMahon, M.O.; Reisch, M. & Patti, R., (1991). *Scholarship in social work: Integration of research, teaching, and service.* National Association of Deans and Directors of Schools of Social Work.

Neugeboren, B. (1988). Field practica in social work administration: Tasks, auspice, selection criteria and outcomes. *Journal of Social Work Education, 24*(2):151-158.

Raphael, F.B. & Rosenblum, A.F. (1987). An operational guide to the faculty field liaison role. *Social Casework: The Journal of Contemporary Social Work*, March:156-163.

Raskin, M.S. (1994). The Delphi study in field instruction revisited: Expert consensus on issues and research priorities. *Journal of Social Work Education, 30*(1):75-88.

Rosenblum, A.F. & Raphael, F.B. (1983). The role and function of the faculty field liaison. *Journal of Education for Social Work, 19*(1):67-73.

Schneck, D. (1991a). Ideal and reality in field education. In D. Schneck, B. Grossman & U. Glassman (Eds.) *Field education in social work: Contemporary issues and trends.* (17-35). Dubuque, Iowa: Kendall/Hunt.

Schneck, D. (1991b). Integration of learning in field education: Elusive goal and educational imperative. In D. Schneck, B. Grossman & U. Glassman (Eds.) *Field education in social work: Contemporary issues and trends.* (67-77). Dubuque, Iowa: Kendall/Hunt.

Smith, H.Y., Faria, G. & Brownstein, C. (1986). Social work faculty in the role of liaison: A field study. *Journal of Social Work Education, 22*(3):68-78.

Tolson, E.R. & Kopp, J. (1988). The practicum: Clients, problems, interventions and influences on student practice. *Journal of Social Work Education, 24*(2):123-134.

Vayda, E. & Bogo, M. (1991). A teaching model to unite classroom and field. *Journal of Social Work Education, 27*(3):271-278.

Wheeler, B.R. & Gibbons, W.E. (1992). Social work in academia: Learning from the past and acting on the present. *Journal of Social Work Education, 28*(3):300-311.

Chapter 9

Linking a Competency-Based Public Child Welfare Curriculum with Field Work: Achieving Agreement About Who is Responsible for Teaching What

Sherrill J. Clark
Kathleen McCormick

T his paper reports on a multi-school, state-wide process using a competency-based curriculum for MSW preparation for the field of public child welfare. Overall co-ordination for the project is provided by the California Social Work Education Center (CalSWEC), a partnership among 12 graduate schools of social work in California and 58 county welfare departments. This paper demonstrates how the competencies provide a basis for structure and collaboration among agency social workers and university faculty. The initial development of the competency-based curriculum, its evolution over four years with emphasis on its use in the field, and the efforts to modify it will be described. The results of three methods used to develop and modify the curriculum will be reported. They are:

1) the Delphi method to initially develop the competency-based curriculum,
2) student focus groups, and
3) a series of community focus groups consisting of practitioners and consumers.

Finally, recommendations are made for adapting this multi-school process to a single-school system and under conditions of financial restraint.

Problem Statement

One of the main stumbling blocks to an articulated learning experience for social work students is a lack of agreement about who is responsible for teaching what. The assumption has been that this lack of agreement is because the classroom and the field have different goals. At their extremes, the agencies believe that universities are not teaching what needs to be taught in order to get the job done, whereas universities believe that agency bureaucracy does not allow for professional practice (Seaberg, 1982; Helfgott, 1991).

We propose that if the field and the school can agree on the notion that practice and education have common goals, they may collaborate to provide diverse learning opportunities as well as good practice. The use of a competency-based curriculum provides the common ground for integrating knowledge obtained in the classroom with skill-building learned or taught in the field and obviates the necessity of a separate field curriculum (Gordon & Gordon, 1982).

Lack of clear expectations may contribute to a lack of planned learning opportunities. When the responsibility for who should be teaching what is unclear, the opportunities to learn can range from planned to serendipitous. Contemporary educational knowledge and practice suggest that theory and practice, reflection and action, belong in both classroom and field environment. In both settings students can be challenged to deal with conceptual and empirical implications as well as the skill demands to rehearse and master content. In the classroom and the field placement, a student can learn these skills: differentiating between behavioral and attitudinal observations, transmitting ideas in terms of another person's frame of reference, and partializing problems (Maier, 1981).

If one is prepared with appropriate values, skills, and knowledge, one can take advantage of opportunities to apply them in the field. If the field is considered an integral part of social work education, then planning for the sequence of knowledge and skill acquisition is important. Often students complain that knowledge learned in the classroom is not relevant to practice in the field, and vice versa, because the sequencing does not occur in the right order or because the field opportunities are missing entirely.

One of the challenges, then, for social work education has been to bring together the learning frame of reference and the practice frame of reference (Gordon & Gordon, 1982). The learning frame of reference encompasses what the student needs to learn, know, value, understand, and do. The practice frame of reference is that which focuses on the interface between the person and the environment. When these two frames of reference are taught together, students can see the field application of the basic principles learned in the classroom without having to determine the framework differences held by their field and classroom teachers.

One perspective has been that the field must have a separate curriculum of its own in order to be relevant to social work practice. Another has stated that the field is an addendum to the classroom experience, or "a special laboratory for the total school curriculum" (Pilcher, 1982). We argue in this paper that the field curriculum is not a supplement to, nor is it separate from, the total school curriculum.

Currently most social work programs rely on the faculty field liaison to integrate classroom learning and field instruction (Royse et al, 1996). The liaison position is key as a boundary spanner between school and agency. Recommendations in this area have focused on how the field liaison or the school can enhance student-field instructor relationships.

There is little direct evidence of the impact of good field instruction on student learning. However, measures of student satisfaction have been used as second-order evidence of good field instruction (Kadushin, 1989). Further, student perception of support from the field instructor has been found to be the primary criterion for student satisfaction in field work (Heppner & H&ly, 1981; Larson & Hepworth, 1982; Fortune et al, 1985). The question remains, however: When the instructor acts a certain way, does the student become an effective professional? At least one study has identified field instructor characteristics that students thought helped them learn; these characteristics included knowledge about the profession, supportiveness, availability for consultation, developing student independence, and providing structure to the learning experience (Urbanowski & Dwyer, 1988).

In the Larson and Hepworth (1982) study, an experimental competency-based/task-centered method of practicum instruction was contrasted with a control group experiencing a traditional method of field instruction. In the experimental group, students performed at a higher level of skill than students who had a traditional practicum focused on case dynamics, rather than student performance using specific skill competencies (p. 53). We also approached the development of a curriculum using competencies relating to skills, knowledge, and values.

Methods and Results

Initial Curriculum Development

The National Association of Public Child Welfare Administrators' survey (1991) of the collaborative efforts of public child welfare agencies and schools of social work encourages the joint development of competency-based assessment of practice. For our curriculum effort, collaboration and specificity of curriculum elements were regarded as primary goals. We believed that if we started with the elements themselves, rather than challenging existing structures in either the university or the agency, we would be able to develop a curriculum that met the needs of both professional graduate social work education and professional child welfare services. The elements are competencies that capable graduate social work specialists in child welfare are expected to know and be able to do.

The main source for the original MSW student competency list was a document developed for child welfare workers at the Institute for Human Services in Columbus, Ohio (Hughes & Rycus, 1987). Additional primary sources were: a list of in-service training competencies developed for the State of California Emergency Response Training Project at California State University at Fresno (Tabbert et al, 1988); and a list of fieldwork competencies developed at California State University, Long Beach (Black et al, 1990). These competencies were modified, supplemented and categorized by the curriculum committee of the Board of CalSWEC and staff, resulting in a proposed list of 126 competencies early in 1991.

In order to accomplish the collaborative implementation of the competency-based curriculum, a partnership among schools of social work and public agencies was first enhanced, maintained, and then encouraged to grow.[2] Consequently, the curriculum committee nominated an advisory group of 30 culturally diverse stakeholders representing public and non-profit social services and university faculty. A modified Delphi method (Delbeq, 1975; Lauffer, 1984), used to poll the advisory group, elicited their opinions about the proposed 126 competencies. A mail poll was chosen to keep travel and time burdens to a minimum and to give equal weight to all respondents' opinions.

By December 1991, the competency list had been reduced to 76 by retaining all competencies which had been nominated as necessary for basic child welfare practice by at least 67 percent of the advisory group.[3] A statewide conference was then held for 100 stakeholders to introduce the competency-based curriculum and a statement of goals and principles.[4] Working in five regional groups, school faculty and agency personnel agreed to adopt the competency-based curriculum and completed three tasks: refinement of the goals and principles, agreement on the three most important competencies representing gaps in the current regional curricula, and discussion of further research needed in public child welfare services (Clark & Grossman, 1992). Since then, CalSWEC project co-ordinators from each of the twelve schools in the coalition have submitted annual curriculum snapshot progress reports evaluating the competency-based curriculum and documenting efforts to close the gaps.

Since the implementation of the competencies, schools have introduced integrated field seminars for the students in the program. These seminars are intended to cover the competencies that are not adequately covered elsewhere in the curriculum. Since each school had its own curriculum before the CalSWEC project, each school had different competencies missing or inadequately covered.[5] This has resulted in twelve different seminars, varying in content depending on the school.

Student Focus Groups

The curriculum was implemented on a limited basis in the spring of 1993. In 1994, nine focus groups were held at each school having graduating MSW students in the CalSWEC program. A total of 71 graduating second-year MSW students (out of 104) participated (68.3%). These students received one-and-one-half years of the two-year curriculum. Because the curriculum was only partially implemented for the first class, that data was used as a pilot study to direct the analysis for the second year. In 1995, 11 focus groups were held at each member school having a graduating class which received the whole curriculum. A total of 137 students (out of 186) were interviewed (73.6%).

Initially, the data were read three times by two authors to conceptualize and label the phenomena that the students were describing. The method described by Strauss and Corbin (1990) was used to develop analytic categories through the grouping of concepts guided by the six sections of the curriculum listed in Table 1 (see p. 136-37). The data were then examined for student opportunities to gain the essential knowledge and skill in the classroom and/or the field in each section[6].

The results were organized in the context of the competency-based curriculum's six sections (Table 1). The most important comment the students made was they need to have the opportunity to apply what they learn in the classroom or else learning is disconnected from their experience in graduate school.

Further, students stated that it was important to get enough clinical experience in the field in order to put their theoretical knowledge to use. They recommended placements be carefully monitored by schools to ensure that students have consistent opportunities to work with a variety of problems and an appropriate mix of simple and complicated cases. Case assignment should be dependent upon an assessment of each individual student's abilities and amount of past experience using the competencies as learning objectives in the student learning agreements. The use of focus groups to elicit information about the curriculum from the students led to the application of this same method to community groups.

Community Focus Groups

Between August and December 1995, 15 focus groups consisting of 131 persons were conducted by university project co-ordinators. Each school conducted at least one focus group with local public child welfare services (CWS) agency representatives such as supervisors, line workers, managers, staff developers, first-year students in the program, graduate CWS workers who had been in the program, former clients, non-profit agency CWS representatives, faculty, probation officers, and lawyers who work within the CWS system.

Most groups were homogeneous. For example, the agency representatives were all from one county or represented one type of stakeholder, e.g., all students, clients, or faculty. Three focus groups called together representatives from different rural Northern California counties. Two focus groups were composed of multiple disciplines (lawyers and supervisors, representatives from probation, non-profit organizations, private practitioners, and different levels of agency representatives). Some groups included line workers, supervisors, and managers.

The participants listed and discussed the five most important knowledge and skill areas they believed were essential for beginning practice in public child welfare. The raw data consisted of individual worksheets from each participant on which they listed the five most highly rated skills and knowledge areas. The group leaders forwarded either a summary of the group's five most highly rated areas or the individual ratings of these areas to the Center. The summaries were not weighted by the number of participants. This was done because a comparison of the five most highly rated areas from the three summarized groups with the five most highly rated areas from the summary of individual tallies showed the same items were included in the same order. When the tally was complete, the items were ordered from the first to the fifth most important areas. Then this list was compared to the CalSWEC competency-based curriculum (Clark & Grossman, 1992).

Tables 2 (see p. 138-39) and 3 (see p. 140-41) list the skill, knowledge, and value areas judged by community focus group participants to be most important for a beginning child welfare worker to know and to be able to do. Important content areas generated in the community focus groups were compatible with the competency-based curriculum.

Community participants identified several areas that needed more specialized attention in the MSW curriculum. For example, "Legal Services and Policies," identified by the community focus groups and addressed by students, had not been originally included in the competency-based curriculum. In Workplace Management some skill items were more specific than the competencies, These included areas such as coping with the stress on the job and multidisciplinary collaboration. These issues were consequently addressed at the Curriculum Modification Conference in the most recent phase of the curriculum development process.

The Curriculum Modification Conference

A two day statewide conference was held in January 1996, to update the original 1991 curriculum. Using the information from the community and student focus groups, participants were charged with four tasks:

1) review the adequacy of the existing competencies;
2) develop better descriptions of how the students would learn each competency or cluster of competencies;

(continued on p. 142)

Table 1
Summary of Student Comments

- Ethnic Sensitive Practice
  - Classroom: Most students indicated they wanted guidance on how institutional factors affect clients, less emphasis on macro aspects of racism and poverty; specific instruction tailoring interventions addressing cultural differences in a manner that respects individual differences.
  - Field: Students indicated the need for a diverse caseload representing a range of problems encountered and increasing levels of difficulty over time.

- Core Child Welfare Skills
  - Classroom: Students wanted more information about the psychosocial and intergenerational aspects of substance abuse; legal issues, including the structure of social services and how a client legally moves from one phase to another.
  - Field: Risk assessment training; practice writing court reports, petitions, and paperwork relating to the emancipation of minors; more exposure to and supervision of cases which involve substance abuse.

- Social Work Skills and Methods
  - Classroom: Students wanted more content on family therapy, interviewing children, how to deal effectively with families in crisis and nonvoluntary clients; methods must balance clinical and case management knowledge and skill presentations. Need instructors with recent experience in the field.
  - Field: Students requested more opportunities to apply clinical judgment in case management situations.

- Human Behavior and the Social Environment
  - Classroom: Students requested more flexibility to choose specialized courses, especially for those who majored in child development as undergraduates or who are experienced child welfare workers. They need in-depth information about the effects of substance abuse and foster care on child and adolescent development in HBSE courses. They need human development information in child abuse and substance abuse classes.
  - Field: They need opportunities to apply knowledge to a variety of cases with varying degrees of difficulty.

- Workplace Management
  - Classroom: Students need more multidisciplinary courses to learn basics of collaboration with other professionals. They also need more on translating theoretical knowledge about organizations into practice in public child welfare.
  - Field: Students stated that nonprofits provide better opportunities for referral and networking skills, while public child welfare offers opportunities to learn consultation skills. They think they need more opportunities to learn how to perform paperwork requirements adequately and more information about how to handle stress and large caseloads.

- Child Welfare Management Skills.
  - Classroom: Students need knowledge of history of social welfare and formation of various policies considered valuable, but also more on the implications of policy for individual clients and advocacy skills to determine the correct courses of action when agency policies conflict with best interest of client.
  - Field: They need a supportive environment to address policy conflicts and resistances in relation to clients' needs.

Table 2
Community Focus Groups — Most Frequently
Promoted Knowledge Competencies for
Beginning Child Welfare Workers

#1 Developmental Issues
- *Child development
- abnormal/normal
- adolescent development
- adult development
- attachment and separation
- effects of illness and developmental disabilities such as HIV and the effects of fetal alcohol syndrome on children and families
- identify abuse and neglect (developmental indicators).
  - effects of child abuse and neglect (physical, emotional, and sexual) on development
- understand the dynamics of incest, sexual abuse

Family development/dynamics/systems
- child and adult mental health issues/DSM IV
- *effects of substance abuse on families
- family development
- foster family issues
- knowledge of healthy parenting, parenting skills
- social histories — know components of
- understanding the impact of domestic violence on the family

#2 Legal and policy issues and politics/Child welfare/legislation/ policies
- understanding of the child welfare laws
- dual role of the protective services social worker
- *understanding the child welfare service delivery system and relationship of NPOs to public child welfare
- know juvenile court process
- family legislation
- federal Indian Child Welfare Act
- history and philosophy of child welfare services (e.g., permanency planning, reasonable efforts, standards of parenting, minimum needs)

- identify abuse and neglect (legal indicators)
- state regulations

#3 Cultural sensitivity
- human diversity
- *self awareness of values and attitudes
- community/family values as they affect definitions of abuse and neglect/influence of culture on community support to the family
- have a realistic understanding of who the clients are/e.g., don't assume that they know how to read or write
- understand the impact of poverty and racism on families

#4 Relationship of public social welfare to other social support systems
- *community resources know and access/how to use in an emergency
- knowledge of organization's policies/bureaucracy
- knowledge of the local county culture, how local system works/ knowledge of local politics
- inter-agency relationships
- intra-agency teams /how organization works
- multidisciplinary teamwork
- need for paperwork

ATTITUDES and VALUES
Social work practice values and ethics/*professional attitudes:
- empathy /be compassionate yet objective
- flexibility to assignment change, willingness to learn, respect confidentiality
- know boundaries
- "neither a prosecutor nor a rescuer be"
- seek continuing education
- understand the differences between case management, clinical intervention, and therapy.

* Starred items indicate the most frequently promoted competency within each group

Table 3
Community Focus Groups — Most Frequently Promoted Skill Competencies for Beginning Child Welfare Workers

#1 Interviewing/Assessment (Fundamental Skills)
- children
- families
- home
- nonvoluntary clients/hostile and/or resistant clients/how to work with lies
- *risk assessment
  - abuse, reabuse, sexual abuse and neglect
  - suicide
  - substance abuse
  - violence
- types of specific interviewing skills
  - crisis intervention
  - doing a home study
  - knowing how to listen and keep focussed
  - keeping own boundaries
  - intake and referral
  - showing nonjudgmental, acceptance of the family
  - taking a social history

#2 Workplace Management issues
- advocacy for clients
- *collaboration/teamwork, team building/ working with multidisciplinary and multiagency teams
- *communication, written and oral/report writing
- computer literacy
- managing stress; burnout and how to avoid it
- street smarts: self-safety and self-protective behaviors
- time management, managing heavy caseloads
- using supervision and consultation with co-workers effectively

#3 Casework/Counseling/Clinical Skills
- assessment of adult mental health
- ability to prioritize goals
- ability to create realistic plans, use consequences, and set limits
- *case management and making referrals
- case planning
- communication
- conflict resolution/negotiation/problem-solving/ critical thinking
- establish positive relationships with the children and the family, engage and motivate
- establish a service network for the family
- identifying family strengths
- selecting the appropriate dispositions

#4 Cultural sensitivity
- culturally responsive interventions
- culturally sensitive assessments
- *developing and maintaining good relationships with the community support systems/outreach

#5 Legal issues and court procedures
- children
- *court/evidentiary report writing
- giving testimony in court
- interacting with court personnel successfully
- making emancipation plans

*   Starred items indicate the most frequently promoted competency within each group

3) determine the sequencing of instruction, make connections explicit between learning in the classroom, practice in the classroom and field, and apply learning to actual situations in the field; and

4) begin to define what level of learning belongs in the graduate program and what level belongs in in-service education.

It was the third task that resulted in suggestions for identifying the learning experiences designed to address each competency that could occur in the field or in the classroom.

The newly revised, competency-based curriculum was approved by the Board in mid-June. Implementation of the new curriculum includes ongoing review of the suggestions made for knowledge and skill-learning experiences in the field and/or in the classroom and the levels of skill required.

Conclusion and Discussion

There have been several benefits and limitations to this process. First, faculty need not completely revise their syllabi to address the competencies. Most of the competencies, although written in the context of preparing public child welfare practitioners, are basic social work skills. Second, the competencies have been used as the basis for learning objectives to help students apply knowledge learned in the classroom to specific field experiences and practitioners are comfortable with the specificity of objectives. Third, field instructors can participate in the curriculum modification process by defining specific field experiences relevant to applying knowledge and building specific skills within the context of the competencies. Finally, in their function as classroom teachers, faculty can connect with the field work experience because the competencies show that there is no exclusive place to learn a competency — only different levels. Each program has to decide what level to provide.

In terms of limitations, the operationalization of the competencies using a consensus building process has been slow to achieve and the creation of the appropriate sequencing with concurrent field work is difficult. Further, calling all stakeholders together can be an expensive process, even if it is done infrequently. It may instead be desirable to encourage small networks of agencies to meet regularly in the context of practice and field instruction.

Finally, there is the danger that program goals can be displaced onto the competencies. One student complained that her field seminar was so full of competencies that were not met elsewhere in the curriculum she did not have a place to process her thoughts about her cases.

Recommendations for Designing A System For Times Of Resource Restraint

Ours is an extensive multi-school, multi-agency program involving an external board with many resources. Short of creating large field units with faculty from the universities, there are efficient ways to design group experiences and introduce economies of scale, which encourage sharing of responsibility for teaching. What are the necessary elements to successfully address the issue of sharing responsibility for teaching and creating opportunities for students that will contribute to a planned learning experience? Our general principle has been the use of a competency-based curriculum in conjunction with frequent involvement of all stakeholders using the new information obtained to modify what is in place.

Recommendations for a Multi-School System

Some methods CalSWEC has employed for a multi-school system have been to:

- Maintain centralized and nurture local structures: Board consisting of agency and university administrators, site project co-ordinators, field liaisons;
- Encourage multi-school field units;
- Reduce field instructors' caseload to supervise students;
- Obtain information from the practice community at regular intervals using the annual report process and attendance at agency administrative meetings;
- Hold occasional conferences among the broad membership of concerned stakeholders, faculty, practitioners and clients;
- Fund curriculum development projects and disseminate them at faculty development institutes, in-service training academies, centralized lending library, distance education programs, and to rural consultants.

Recommendations for a Single School System

Some suggestions for a single school system focusing on collaboration between school and field have been:

- Involve the school and the agency administrators at regular planned intervals to review the curriculum;
- Identify the field liaison as the key boundary spanner. Hold meetings with field liaisons from other schools;
- Hold curriculum review workshops for field instructors in which to define the learning objectives in terms of the competencies and identify field learning opportunities for the students. Make sure they take something concrete away with them and that they know exactly how the school will back up skill-building for practice with knowledge acquired in the classroom;
- Plan for recognition ceremonies at the end of the school year and build in an evaluation component, specifically evaluating the learning opportunities;
- Obtain yearly input from the faculty, the field and the students. Use the focus group method or other exploratory method at least until all the important categories have been identified (Morgan, 1993);
- Pool resources with other schools in the same region for holding faculty development institutes in which the field and classroom faculty meet;
- Encourage students to request specific learning experiences and support their ability to be assertive about this;
- Provide integrative seminars across field work agencies, especially agencies that form referral networks among themselves with respect to practice (Marshack & Glassman, 1991).

In this system, second-year students should be held accountable for identifying their own learning needs. At some point in their student careers, they realize they have a finite amount of time left and begin developing a continuing education plan. Using a competency-based curriculum upon which all agree makes it easier for students to identify and ask for specific experiences. It should not be seen as a failure of the school if it does not define all the learning experiences in the curriculum, but it is the school's responsibility to provide the opportunities.

Expect changes to occur in small steps and expect the curriculum to evolve. Any success can be built upon using a collaborative system, but the schools must be responsive to small changes. To adequately prepare graduates for current workplace realities, social work educators have had to design curricula specific enough to be relevant to practice, while remaining broad enough to offer a professional education.

Endnotes

1   The authors wish to thank Bart Grossman, Field Director, for his support for the student focus group project and help on the literature review; and Lisa Tracy, doctoral student researcher, for her assistance on the first year of the student focus group project. Both are from the School of Social Welfare, University of California at Berkeley.

2   As the curriculum has been implemented, schools have made efforts to include community stakeholders such as other professionals, foster parents, and clients.

3   Less than two percent of the competencies were rated as unnecessary by the advisory group. The rest were rated as desirable, but not necessary for beginning practice.

4   The competency-based curriculum is available upon request from the California Social Work Education Center, School of Social Welfare, University of California at Berkeley, 120 Haviland Hall, Berkeley CA 94720. Soon it will be available on line at our Web site.

5   The CalSWEC project funds an additional classroom full time equivalent for every 20 stipended students in the program.

6   Because the 1995 database consisted of 260 pages of transcripts, a qualitative data analysis computer program (NUD*IST) was used to assist with the analysis.

References

Black, J., Hughes, T., & Crose, J. *Fundamental and specialized child welfare competencies.* Handouts from "Building child welfare practitioners." Anaheim, CA, October 5, 1990.

Bogardus, E. (1921). *Methods of training social workers.* Los Angeles, CA: Southern California Sociological Society.

Clark, S. & Grossman, B. (1992). *The California competency-based child welfare curriculum project.* Berkeley, CA: CalSWEC.

Delbeq, A., Van den Ven, A., 7 Gustafson, D. (1975). *Group techniques for program planning: A guide to nominal group and Delphi processes.* Glenview, IL: Scott, Foresman & Co.

Fortune, A. et al., (1985). Students' satisfaction with field placements. *Journal of Social Work Education, 21*(3):92-104.

Gordon, W. & Gordon, M. (1991). The role of frames of reference in field instruction. In Sheafor, B. 7 Jenkins, L. *Quality field instruction in social work: Program development & maintenance.* New York: Longman.

Grossman, B. (1987). The heritage & challenge of social field instruction. Adapted from a paper presented at the Annual Conference on Field Instruction. Arizona State University, Tempe, Arizona, August 20th.

Helfgott, K. (1991). *Staffing the child welfare agency: Recruitment & retention.* Washington, DC: Child Welfare League of America.

Heppner, P. 7 Handly, P. (1981). A study of the interpersonal influence process in supervision. *Journal of Counseling Psychology, 28*(5):437-444.

Hughes, R. & Rycus, J. (1989). *Target: Competent staff.* Washington D.C. and Columbus, OH: Child Welfare League of America and the Institute of Human Services.

Kadushin, A. (1989). What is qualitatively different about quality field education? Paper delivered at the Council of Social Work Education Annual Program meeting, March, 1989.

Larson, J. & Hepworth, D. (1982). Enhancing the effectiveness of practicum instruction. *Journal of Education for Social Work, 13*(2):50-58.

Lauffer, A. (1984). *Strategic marketing for not-for-profit organizations.* New York, NY: Free Press.

Maier, H. (1981). Chance favors the prepared mind. *Contemporary Social Work Education, 4*(1):14-20.

Marshack, E. & Glassman, U. (1991). Innovative models for field instruction: Departing from traditional models. In Schneck, D., Grossman, B. & Glassman, U. *Field education in social work: Contemporary issues and trends.* Dubuque, IA: Kendall/Hunt.

Morgan, D. (1993). *Successful focus groups: Advancing the state of the art.* Newbury Pk, CA: Sage.

National Association of Public Child Welfare Administrators. (1991). *Public child welfare agencies and schools of social work: The current status of collaboration.* Washington, D.C.: Author.

Pilcher, A. (1991). The development of field instruction objectives. In Sheafor, B. & Jenkins, L. *Quality field instruction in social work: Program development and maintenance.* New York: Longman.

Reynolds, B. C. (1942). *Learning and teaching in the practice of social work.* New York, NY: Rinehart & Company.

Royse, D. (1996). *Field instruction: A guide for social work students* (2nd Edition). White Plains, NY: Longman.

Seaberg, J. (1982). Getting there from here: Revitalizing child welfare training. *Social Work,* (September).

Schneck, D. (1991). Integration of learning in field education: Elusive goal and education imperatives. In Schneck, D., Grossman, B. & Glassman, U. *Field education in social work: Contemporary issues and trends.* Dubuque, IA: Kendall/Hunt.

Strauss, A. & Corbin, J. (1990). *Basics of qualitative research: Grounded theory procedures and techniques.* Newbury Pk, CA: Sage.

Tabbert, W., Sullivan, P., & Whittaker, R. (1988). An empirical validation of competencies required for child protective services practice. Draft Report. California State University, Fresno: Author.

Tolson, E. & Kopp, J. (1988). The practicum: Clients, problems, interventions and influences on student practice. *Journal of Social Work Education,* 2:123-134.

Urbanowski, M. & Dwyer M. (1988). *Learning through field instruction: A guide for teachers and students.* Milwaukee, WI: Family Service of America.

Chapter 10

The Role of Field Education in Preparing Social Work Students for the New Realities of Health Care Practice

Ron Levin
Margot Herbert
Butch Nutter

The health care system is undergoing profound structural change in every part of Canada. Cost containment is the major motivation for these changes, and constant emphasis on the bottom line has contributed to the current focus on shorter hospital stays, ambulatory treatment, blurring of professional roles, regionalization, mergers of health care institutions, program-based management, downsizing of human resources, contracting out of services, etc. Also some of those who fund, plan, and deliver health care services have recognized that the determinants of health extend beyond medical services to include adequate housing, clean air, appropriate educational opportunities, financial security, and standards of community care for vulnerable populations. Although in most provinces there is still little evidence that these ideas are actually being put into place, this may change as the fiscal benefits of this health promotion approach become apparent. In some cases this vision of a comprehensive health system has led to a shift of emphasis from tertiary high tech care to primary, community-based care, with multi- sectoral involvement in planning, and acknowledgment of the consumer as an active partner in the decision making process.

This combination of events has major implications for social work in health care. For example, in some parts of the country the traditional hospital social work department, with its hierarchical structure, has become a thing of the past and many hospitals no longer have social work director positions (CASWAH 1996, Nutter, Levin, & Herbert, 1995). Increasingly, social workers in acute treatment hospitals are assigned to specific programs and report to a program head who is probably not a social worker. Community Health Centres in Ontario, Manitoba, Alberta, etc., CLSC's in Quebec, Hospitals without Walls in New Brunswick are just some examples of various alternate delivery models. In many settings, social workers have had to become quite creative in their attempts to keep their professional heads above water, and those who are unwilling or unable to adapt their practice to participate in radically altered health settings may be declared redundant. If social workers are to become major players in the new health environment, they must be willing (a) to re-examine their roles, functions and skills, and (b) to abandon non-productive ways of working. Jansson and Salisido (1985), Walker and Mitchell (1995), Levin and Herbert (1995), Rosenberg (1994), Simmons (1994), and Levin and Page (1991) have suggested that social workers must improve their brokerage, education, team-building and conflict-resolution skills; become more organizationally astute; and be prepared to conceptualize and put into practice new roles such as resource developer, innovator, and coalition builder. Perhaps most important, social workers in modern health care settings must reclaim their professional roots in advocacy and traditional community development.

A recent study (Herbert & Levin, 1995) indicated that many social workers in health settings believe that they are not adequately prepared for today's practice demands and, therefore, may be emphasizing outmoded functions and roles. Some of these workers, by virtue of their experience and seniority, serve as field instructors and role models for practicum students, perhaps perpetuating the status quo, rather than preparing their students for the health settings in which those students will find employment.

This study reports on the results of a survey that was undertaken to investigate whether field education co-ordinators in Canadian schools of social work perceive that there have been significant recent changes in the hospitals or other health settings where their students do field placements. Respondents who are aware of such changes were asked to comment on the effect of these changes on social work practice and the preparation that students now undertake and should receive in order to practice social work.

Method

Roxanne Power, Associate Practicum Co-ordinator, Faculty of Social Work, University of Toronto, supplied the names, phone and fax numbers for the Field Education Co-ordinators (FEC) in most of the BSW and MSW programs in Canada. The CASSW guide was used to obtain the others. A cover was faxed along with the questionnaire to each FEC asking them to fax back the completed questionnaire. One week later a reminder or thank-you letter was faxed to each of the FECs. This was followed a week later with reminder phone calls to the English programs. English programs received the covering letter and questionnaire in English. French programs received French covering letters and questionnaires in both French and English. In all, 31 programs were contacted, 24 English and seven French. Completed questionnaires were received from 17 English and three French programs, 17 with BSW students placed in hospital/health practicum settings and 12 with MSW students placed in hospital/health settings. All of these programs indicated that they did place students in hospital/health settings practica.

Results

Fourteen programs indicated total numbers of 782 BSW and 449 MSW students in placement during January 1996. One eighth (12%) of these BSW students and one fifth (21%) of these MSW students were placed in departments with a social work director and perhaps one or two supervisors to whom front-line workers report. "Changed" settings were identified as those in which social workers are assigned to specific medically defined programs and report to a team leader who is usually not a social worker.

The pattern of placements was substantially different for BSW and MSW students. As Table 1 shows, nearly two thirds (64%) of BSW students in hospital/health placements were in changed settings and only one third (36%) were in traditional hospital/health settings. However, nearly three fifths (60%) of MSW students were reported to be in traditional settings and only two fifths (40%) in changed hospital/health settings. One fairly large MSW program did not indicate whether its students were placed in traditional or changed settings. However, even if all that program's MSW students were placed in changed settings, MSW students would still have been significantly less likely than BSW students to have been placed in changed settings.

Table 1 BSW and MSW Students in Traditional and Changed Hospital/Health Field Placements*			
Type of Setting	BSW students	MSW students	Total
Traditional	32 (36%)	55 (60%)	87
Changed	58 (64%)	36 (40%)	94
Total	90	91	181

* One program reported that all its students in hospital/health placements were in both traditional and changed placements.

Changes in Hospital/Health Settings

FECs in 17 programs responded that there had been significant changes in the last five years in the hospital/health settings where their students were placed. Their responses were initially coded into the 22 categories. These categories were reduced to the six presented in Table 2. Categories and the responses included in them are:

- Changes in hospitals: hospitals shut/amalgamated, more competition with nursing, more contracts versus permanent jobs, lay-offs/fewer social workers, cuts in resources, bed closures, more stress/uncertainty/anxiety, and regionalization
- Changes within social work departments: social work directors/social work departments gone, program management, less social work identity/supervision, more hiring of BSW versus MSWs, administrators gone, restructuring/reorganizing social work services
- Changes in patient population: increase in aging population, more acute care needs
- Changes in social work practice: shorter patient stays, more crisis intervention

- Changes in the nature of social work placements: more community health placements, fewer placements
- Change uncertain: changes now occurring — results unclear, little change in social work functions.

Table 2
Changes in Hospital/Health Field Placement Settings
During the Last Five Years

Types of changes	Count	Percent of cases[*]
In hospitals	26	144.4
Within social work departments	18	100.0
In patient population	3	16.7
In social work practice	3	16.7
Nature of social work placements	2	11.1
Change uncertain	2	11.1
Total	54	300.0

[*]   18 valid cases, each of which gave up to seven responses

Note that in Table 2, FECs mentioned up to seven changes each. The most frequently mentioned category of changes was the changes in hospitals (26). This was followed by changes to social work departments (18). There were substantially fewer mentions of change in the patient population (3), to social work practice (3), or to the nature of the placements (2). One FEC indicated that the changes were just beginning and their results were unclear. Another FEC said there were reorganizational shifts in respect to persons and reporting structures, "however, minimal change in terms of social work functions."

Social workers' functioning

FECs were asked, "Do you think the social workers who supervise students in hospital/health setting are functioning differently as practitioners than they were five years ago?" Of the 16 FECs who answered this question,

13 chose "Yes" and 3 chose "No." Those who answered "Yes" were asked "If yes, in what ways are they now functioning differently?" Their responses were initially placed in 21 categories. These were further reduced to the five categories displayed in Table 3.

Table 3
Changes in Social Workers Functioning

Types of changes	Count	Percent of cases*
Nature of social work practice	24	160
Type of social work practice	10	67
Patient treatment	4	27
Experience of job	3	20
Don't know yet	2	13
Total	43	287

*   15 valid cases. One FEC who indicated no change, listed a change.

The five response categories in Table 3 included the following more detailed response categories:

- Changes in the nature of social work practice: more ethical dilemmas, larger case-loads, less responsive to patients, less social work identity/supervision, more complex work environment, more accountability, lower on hierarchy, more involvement in multidisciplinary teams, different structure, same work, more autonomous, more program-based decision making, not as much time for students
- Changes to the type of social work practice: emphasis on discharge planning, narrower role, intake, increased advocacy responsibilities, changes in approach to care, more community/family practice, more short term and crisis oriented practice, new areas of service
- Changes in patient treatment: shorter patient stays
- Changes in the experience of the job: more stress, concerned about layoffs, peer morale
- Changes uncertain: don't know yet

Special preparation for *new* hospital/health settings

FECs were then asked, "Do you think students require any special preparation for work in the *new* hospital/health settings." Those 14 who ticked "Yes" were then asked, "If yes, what special preparation should they have?" Thirteen FECs gave suggestions about the type of preparation students needed to work in the *new* hospital/health settings. These responses were initially coded into 22 categories and then reduced to the three categories shown in Table 4.

Table 4
Suggestions for Special Student Preparation to Work in the New Hospital/health Settings

Types of preparation	Count of cases	Percent of cases*
Work climate	18	138.5
Practice knowledge and skill	11	84.6
Other	5	38.5
Total	34	261.6

* 13 valid cases, each of whom could make up to seven suggestions

---

The categories of work climate, practice knowledge and skill, and other include the following more detailed response categories with respect to preparation of students:

- Work climate: intensity and stress, autonomous/independent practice, flexible and clear roles, interdisciplinary settings, team work, multidisciplinary, changes in organizational functional structures — program management, maintaining professional identity in changing environment, using supervision more creatively
- Practice knowledge and skill: values and ethics, diversity/anti-oppressive practice, advocacy, aging, history of health care, social work registration act, course on health care settings, multi-cultural/ethnic practice, working with communities, preparation specific to practicum

- Other: field instructors need more preparation, unsure, shift from clinical preference, don't know yet, in-setting student support seminars

Most of these FECs seemed to think that BSW and MSW students need more preparation than they are currently receiving to deal with a more exposed work climate. Their responses indicated that students should be better prepared in terms of social work identity in order to work within a multidisciplined setting where there is typically not the same social work departmental dynamic that has existed in the past.

Modifications to current course work

FECs were then asked, "Do you think the current course work at your institution needs to be modified to prepare students for the new hospital/ health settings?" Those ticking "Yes" were further asked, "If yes, what modifications to course work are needed?" Ten FECs offered more or less specific suggestions for content. Most (eight) indicated that the material they were suggesting should be included in current courses rather than take the form of additional courses. Their suggestions were initially coded into 20 categories that were then reduced to the four categories presented in Table 5.

Table 5
Material to be Added to Courses to Prepare Students to Work in the *New* Hospital/health Settings

Types of material	Count	Percent of cases*
Work climate	10	111
Practice knowledge and skill	10	111
Other	2	22
Put content into existing courses	8	89
Total	30	333

* 10 valid cases, each of whom could give up to seven responses

---

The four categories of material presented in Table 5 were reduced from the following more detailed categories of responses:

- Work climate: autonomous/independent practice, flexible & clear role, inter-disciplinary settings, team work, organizational functional structures–program management, redefine health away from sickness model, professionalism in changing environment
- Practice knowledge and skill: values & ethics, diversity/anti-oppressive practice, advocacy, aging, community strategies/interventions, poverty and health, social work registration act, working with communities
- Other: "New" applies to all social work practice, unsure, being addressed now
- Put content into existing courses

Not surprisingly, these responses were much like the responses about what additional preparation students needed to work in the new hospital/health settings. It is interesting to note that at least one of these FECs thinks that what is happening in the new hospital/health settings is happening in all social work practice.

Information about practice issues

FECs were next asked, "As a field co-ordinator, do you identify practice issues (such as organizational and practice changes in hospital/health settings) to your colleagues who plan and develop course material (such as Social Work Methods courses)?" Of the 14 who answered this question, nine ticked "Yes" and five ticked "No." Those ticking "Yes" were then asked, "How do you gather the information?" Responses from ten FECs were initially placed in 11 categories that were subsequently reduced to the four shown in Table 6.

All of the FECs indicated that they received information about practice issues from Field Instructors, usually (eight) through informal discussions, in one case from Field Instructor forms, and in another case from discussions with administrators. Most also received information from students. Three received their information from students through informal discussions, another three through integrative seminars, and one by student evaluations of their field placements. "Other" sources of information were media and other reports, community networking, and ad hoc. Information from faculty

Table 6
Field Education Co-ordinators' Sources of Information
About Practice Issues to Share with Their Colleagues

Sources of information	Count	Percent of cases*
Field Instructors	12	120
Students	7	70
Other	5	50
Colleagues	3	30
Total	27	270

* 9 FECs ticked yes, but 10 listed ways they gathered information about practice issues.

colleagues came through informal discussions and from faculty field liaisons. These results provide little evidence of systematic efforts to discover practice issues associated with social work student field placements. Respondents were also asked, "How do you disseminate that information to your colleagues?" Responses to this question are shown in Table 7.

Table 7
How Field Education Co-ordinators Share Information About
Practice Issues with Their Colleagues

Sources of information	Count of cases	Percent of cases*
Informal discussion	6	60
Faculty participate in the field and share their information	4	40
Faculty meetings	4	40
Formal curriculum reviews	4	40
Field instructors participate in faculty	2	20
When planning course content	1	10
Total	21	210

* 9 FECs ticked yes, but 10 listed ways they shared information about practice issues.

There does not appear to be formal mechanisms or procedures for FECs to share information about practice issues with colleagues who are preparing and teaching courses to students. In many schools of social work, many faculty are officially involved in field instruction in the capacities of faculty field liaison. However, in some schools, faculty field liaisons do not make field visits unless there is a problem. This appears, at best, to be an unreliable way of a faculty keeping updated on practice issues.

Courses — Required, Optional, and Not Offered

One aspect of interest was the courses that faculties might be offering or requiring that would provide knowledge about some of the practice issues that students confront when placed in hospital/health settings. We asked, "Please indicate in which of the following topic areas courses are required, optional, or not offered for students who you place in hospital/ health settings:" This was followed by a list of 10 courses listed first in Table 8.

Of the courses listed, research was most likely (19 of 20 schools) to be required of students placed in hospital/health care settings. Perhaps surprising, none of these schools required students placed in hospital/health care settings to take a course on hospital/health social work, and only 13 offered such a course as an option.

Respondents were then asked, "Are there additional courses that should be offered in your social work program to better prepare students for practice in hospital/health settings?" Eleven ticked "Yes" and nine ticked "No." They were then instructed, "If yes, what are they and should they be required or optional?" The second part of Table 8 lists the courses that the FECs would add to their curricula for students placed in hospital/health settings. Many of these reflect the kinds of changes that these FECs expressed earlier in the questionnaire.

Innovations to prepare students for hospital/health placements

Finally, FECs were asked, "Are you doing anything particularly innovative or different in your field education program to prepare students for practice in hospital/health settings?" Of the 16 who answered this question, seven ticked "Yes." They were asked, "If yes, please describe these innovations."

Table 8
Courses Required, Optional, or Not Offered to Students In
Hospital/health Field Placements

Current course offerings	Required	Optional	Not Offered
Hospital/health social work		13	6
Community social work	10	8	2
Administration/organizational behaviour	6	10	4
Research	19	1	
Multicultural/ethnic social work	3	14	3
Social work supervision	1	2	17
Social work with groups	6	13	1
Social policy	18	1	
Human behaviour & development	13	1	6
Program evaluation	5	4	11
Courses that should be added			
Hospital/health social work	1	1	
Administration		1	
Multicultural/ethnic social work		2	
Social work supervision		1	
Human behaviour & development	1	1	
Program evaluation		2	
Interdisciplinary practice		1	
Professional role, values & ethics	1		
The new "medical" social work		1	
Community practice & health care		1	
Palliative care		1	
Multi/interdisciplinary teams		1	
Social work and the aging		1	

The innovations described by these respondents, along with their frequencies are listed in Table 9.

Table 9
Innovations for Preparing Students for Hospital/health Field Placements

Innovative methods	Count [*]
Speakers from placements present to students	1
Interdisciplinary non-credit course developed by faculty from several disciplines and taken by students from several disciplines	1
Students have structured interdisciplinary days	1
New curriculum with orientation, seminars, interviews, and courses	2
Seminars with practitioners	1
Newsletter, not specific to health	1
Student orientation	1
Changes planned for Fall 1996	1
Hospitals provide seminars for students and field instructors, system orientations, interdisciplinary rounds, and educational experiences	1
More group supervision where students can share their experiences	1
Two supervisors for each student in placement	1
Total	12

[*] Each of the seven FECs who said they were doing something innovative could list more than one innovation.

Discussion And Implications

It is evident from the responses provided by field education co-ordinators across Canada that they are aware of and concerned about the changes that are taking place within the health care delivery system and the implications of those changes for social work education and training. These changes have been reported both in relation to the context for social work practice, as well as the nature of social work practice. Many social workers are now working within reconstituted organizations and are no longer part of social work departments. Therefore, opportunities previously available for supervision and mentoring no longer exist. Also, since in-patients are often sicker and discharged more quickly, social work practice is increasingly focused on crisis intervention, instrumental assistance, discharge planning, and community-oriented practice. Some practitioners and authors (Rosenberg, 1996; Herbert & Levin, 1995) predict that the future of social work in health care may lie outside the institution.

Three-quarters of the respondents acknowledged that students should receive additional preparation for the new health care environment in the form of additional content integrated into existing courses or through new courses added to current curricula. Existing classroom and field instruction are unlikely to produce graduates adequately prepared to practice effectively in the new health care system. Currently a third of the schools in this survey did not offer a course in hospital/health care practice even though they all place students in health care settings. The schools that did offer hospital/ health care courses do not require students in hospital/health care placements to take these courses. Furthermore, only one-third of the schools represented in this survey require students to take courses in organizational behaviour or administration, and four schools do not offer these courses at all. Levin and Page (1991), Jansson and Simmons (1986), and Berger (1991) have pointed out that workers in health care must have well-developed organizational skills in order to cope with today's climate of constant change. Therefore, it is crucial that this content be provided to all social work students, but particularly to those who are placed in hospitals and other health settings.

Another concern highlighted by the results of this survey relates to the collection and distribution of information concerning health care practice. This is an especially important issue since the field is evolving so rapidly. At present, most field education co-ordinators are informed about changes informally by field instructors and/or students during field visits and classroom discussion. Apparently there is no systematic data gathering process in place to ensure that the information is up-to-date, comprehensive, and accurate. Similarly, only seven of the twelve field education co-ordinators who responded to this question indicated that they informed their classroom colleagues about field developments. Even when this was done, it apparently occurred informally with no structured process in place. While some sessional classroom instructors may work in health care settings, or faculty members may serve as field liaisons for those settings, this is not a certainty and consequently the information imparted to students may be outdated. It is crucial that a systematic process be instituted by FECs to gather up-to-date information about field developments and to distribute that information to classroom instructors.

The results of this research point out potential shortcomings related to future field instruction in hospital/health practice settings. At present, most MSW students in hospital/health settings are being placed in traditional social work departments. This is out of step with the growing trend toward program management.Upon graduation, these students are more likely than BSW graduates to be assigned senior responsibilities and to serve as field instructors (Levin & Herbert, 1995). Therefore, it is imperative that MSW students have opportunities to learn about non-traditional organizational arrangements from field instructors who are functioning successfully in those environments. Also, only seven respondents reported that they had introduced innovations to prepare students for the changes in health care. These focused on providing didactic content including an interdisciplinary non-credit course developed by faculty and students from several disciplines, as well as various seminars presented by practitioners. It appears that to date little attention has been devoted to field placements themselves. This should be a priority for field education co-ordinators who should carefully consider the skills that will best prepare students for future practice through consultation with faculty/field liaisons and agency-based field instructors. The goal is to design creative placements where students can acquire skills for the present and future. For example, in a pilot project currently underway in an Australian school of social work, students are placed simultaneously in a hospital, a community health centre, and a home care setting to ensure that they are able to follow a client from home, into the hospital, and into the community. In this way the student is able to learn about non-institutional care models and to develop linkage, coalition-building, and community organizational skills that might not have been possible if he/she had been placed in only one setting (Brown 1996).

The implications for social work education are clear. In the face of major structural changes across fields of practice, schools of social work should be planning and implementing changes in the content of related academic course material, as well as developing field work opportunities that will prepare students to work in a radically changed practice context. In addition, all schools should develop a formal mechanism by which field education personnel can share local practice developments with their classroom colleagues. This process would enhance the ability of classroom instructors to remain current at a time when constant change is the norm.

References

Berger, C. (1993) *Restructuring & resizing strategies for social work and other human service organizations*. American Hospital Association.

Connections: Newsletter. Canadian Association of Social Work Administrators in Health Facilities. October, 1995.

Herbert, M. & Levin, R. (1995). Current issues and future directions in hospital social work. *The Social Worker, 63* (2): 89-93.

Herbert, M. & Levin, R. (1996). The advocacy role in hospital social work. *Social Work in Health Care, 22* (3): 71-83.

Jansson, B.S., & Salisido, R. (1985). Community practices in health care. In Taylor, S.H. & Roberts R. W. (Eds.) *Theory & practice of community work*. New York: Columbia University Press.

Jansson & Simmons (1986). The survival of social work units in host organizations. *Social Work, 31*(5): 339-343.

Levin, R. & Herbert, M. (1995). *The move to community health centres: Implications for social work practice*. Unpublished paper presented at International Conference for Community Health Centres: At the Centre of Health Care Reform. Montreal, Canada.

Levin R., & Herbert, M. (1995). Differential worker assignments for social work practitioners in hospitals. *Health & Social Work, 20* (1): 21-30.

Levin R. & Page L. (1991). Strategies for developing the organizationally astute medical social worker. In Taylor P., & Devereux, J. (Eds.) *Social work administrative practice in health care settings*. 145-158. Toronto: Canadian Scholars Press.

Nutter, B., Levin, R., & Herbert, M. (1995). The trend to program management in hospitals: Implications for social work education. In Rogers, G. (Ed.) *Social work field education*. (51-74). Dubuque, Iowa: Kendall/Hunt Publishing.

Rosenberg, G. (1994). Social Work, the family and the community. *Social Work in Health Care, 20*(1): 7 - 17.

Rosenberg, G. (1996). *Community care network development*. Unpublished paper presented at Society for Social Work Administrators in Health Care 31st Annual Meeting. Kansas City, Mo.

Simmons, J. (1994). Community based care: The new health social work paradigm. *Social Work in Health Care, 20*(1): 35-46.

Walker, R. & Mitchell, S. (1995). Community-based health care: A different approach to health outcomes. *Australian Health Review, 18*(4): 2-14.

Personal communication (1996) with Prue Brown, Field Education Co-ordinator, University of Melbourne, School of Social Work, Melbourne, Australia.

About the Contributors

Helen Szewello Allen, HBSW, MSW is an Assistant Professor and Coordinator of Field Education at the School of Social Work and Family Studies, University of British Columbia. Previously, she was the Director of Field Education at the McGill University School of Social Work. Her research interests are in field education, refugee issues and prior learning assessment and recognition. She has recently published a study entitled "An Examination of Field Education in Child Welfare in British Columbia."

Marion Bogo, MSW, Adv Dip SW is Professor and Sandra Rotman Chair in Social Work at the Faculty of Social Work, University of Toronto. She is the former Acting Dean, Associate Dean, and was Practicum Coordinator from 1979–1992. She has published extensively on field education, including numerous articles in international journals and *The Practice of Field Instruction in Social Work* (1998, 2nd edition, co-author). Professor Bogo has been invited as guest lecturer and consultant to Schools of Social Work in Canada, the United States, and Asia, particularly Japan and Sri Lanka. Currently she is Principal Investigator on a Social Sciences and Humanities Research Council project that investigates the impact of organizational re-structuring on field education.

Paul Cappuccio, BA, MSW, CSW received his BA in Psychology from York University and his Master of Social Work from the University of Toronto. Currently, Paul is Coordinator of Mental Health Ambulatory Services at Humber River Regional Hospital in Toronto; he has worked as a therapist in their Mood Disorder Program for several years. A social worker for 15 years, he maintains a private practice involving counselling, consultation and capacity assessments. As well Paul has lectured on such topics as grief work, psychotherapy, depression and stress reduction.

Sherrill J. Clark, LCSW, PhD is the Executive Director of the California Social Work Education Center at the University of California at Berkeley. She has been responsible for implementing a California-wide competency-based curriculum to prepare MSWs for work in public child welfare practice. Her research interests include child welfare, health policy, and social work education, especially the continuum of education and practice and how learning in the classroom is transferred to and from the field.

Patrick Clifford, BA, BSW, BEd, MSW, CSSW is a clinical social worker at York County Hospital in Newmarket, Ontario. He is currently the team social worker for The Arthritis Program and a clinician with the Adult Brief Therapy Program/Mental Health Program in York County. He has been a field instructor for Ryerson Polytechnic University, Wilfred Laurier University and Seneca College. He is active in clinical research, a member of several community boards and serves as the professional practice leader for the social work staff at York County Hospital.

Judy Globerman, PhD is an Associate Professor in the Faculty of Social Work at the University of Toronto and the Status of Women Officer for the university. She holds a BSW from the University of Manitoba, a Master of Health Science, Health Care Practice degree from McMaster University and Master of Science and PhD degrees in Community Health from the Faculty of Medicine, University of Toronto. Dr. Globerman's program of research includes research in health care with projects examining the impact of organizational restructuring on social work, family care of persons with Alzheimer's Disease. She is currently the Principal Investigator on a SSHRC study on adaptation of children and families to childhood chronic illness.

Margot Herbert, MSW, RSW is associate professor emeritus, University of Calgary, Faculty of Social Work. She has published in the areas of child welfare, advocacy and medical social work. She continues to teach and consult to various human service organizations.

Gail I. Kenyon, MSW, CSW has been the Field Education Coordinator at Ryerson Polytechnic University School of Social Work, Toronto since 1988. She has published in the areas of field instructor training and the gender income gap among social workers. She has recently accepted a teaching position at East Carolina University in Greenville, North Carolina.

Ron Levin, MSW, RSW is associate professor and head of the Edmonton Division, University of Calgary, Faculty of Social Work. His primary research interests are in medical social work, social work administration, occupational social work and social work education and training. He has written, taught and practiced in these areas.

Kathleen McCormick, MSW, MPH has worked in the substance abuse field since 1985, primarily with populations that are indigent and marginalized. In 1992 she decided to further pursue her education, receiving an MPH and MSW. She is presently working toward her doctorate in Social Welfare at UC Berkeley with a focus on how research on substance use problems informs policy and practice. Presently she is the Substance Abuse Specialist for STRIDES of Alameda County, an assertive community treatment program for persistently mentally ill adults.

Ellen Sue Mesbur, MSW, Ed.D is a Professor at the School of Social Work, Ryerson Polytechnic University. She served as Director of the School for nine years and was one of the founders of the Canadian Field Education network within the Canadian Association of Schools of Social Work.

Jeanne Michaud, MSW graduated from Laval University (Ste-Foy, Québec) in 1970 with a Masters degree in Social Work. She worked as a social worker in the health field and in a rehabilitation center for girls before she started working as a youth worker in 1983, in the Québec Social Services Center. She assumed the task of Field Instructor on a full-time basis from 1990 to 1998 in the Young Offenders Prgram. Still working in that program, she is now her directorate's representative on the team that oversees field instruction in Québec Youth Center, University Institute.

Nona Moscovitz, MSW obtained her Master of Social Work degree from McGill University, Montreal, Quebec. She has been working at the CLSC René-Cassin (community health and social service center) in Montreal since 1993. She is acting coordinator of the Social Gerontology Services, which include an elder abuse team and a mental health team for older adults (60+). Between 1993 and 1997, Nona coordinated the Student Seminar Program under the direction of the Department of Professional Services along with her other responsibilities as a clinical practitioner in the field of mental health.

Richard (Butch) Nutter, PhD, RSW is professor emeritus, University of Calgary, Faculty of Social Work. He has published extensively in the areas of program evaluation, child welfare and addictions.

Roxanne Power, BSW, MSW has been teaching at the Faculty of Social Work, University of Toronto, for 16 years and has been associated with their field education programme for 11 years. At present she is the principal and co-investigator in two funded studies to explore the impact of the changing world of work and its implications for field education.

Gayla Rogers, PhD is professor and dean, Faculty of Social Work, University of Calgary. She has pursued her interest in field education through research, presentations and publications. She has developed and taught courses, seminars and workshops to students and field instructors and has provided consultation to social work programs in Canada, the United States, Australia, the United Kingdom and New Zealand. Gayla has presented and published extensively on field education.

Glen Schmidt, BA, BSW, MSW is an Assistant Professor and Director of Field Education in the social work program at the University of Northern British Columbia. His social work practice experience is largely in the fields of child welfare and mental health in northern and remote communities. He lives in Prince George, British Columbia.

Barbara Thomlison, PhD, is a professor in the School of Social Work and Director of the Institute for Children and Families at Risk at Florida International University. She obtained her PhD in social work from the Univerity of Toronto and has a lengthy interdisciplinary practice history with children, families and policy services research. Her academic interests include child welfare, foster care, mental health, field education, program evaluation, and family interventions. Her current research projects are in the area of school readiness, kinship care and online social work field and practice-based learning. Dr. Thomlison is actively involved as a board and community member in local and national child welfare and family service organizations.